TWENTIETH-CENTURY APOSTLES

TWENTIETH-CENTURY APOSTLES

Contemporary Spirituality in Action

Phyllis Zagano

A Liturgical Press Book

THE LITURGICAL PRESS
Collegeville, Minnesota

Cover design by David Manahan, O.S.B.

The author and publisher are grateful to the following parties for permission to publish the photos of the subjects of *Twentieth-Century Apostles* in this book:

Little Sisters of Jesus (Charles de Foucauld)
Fondation Teilhard de Chardin (Pierre Teilhard de Chardin)
Catholic News Service (Giovanni Battista Montini, Dorothy Day, Jean Vanier [Bill Wittman])
Sheed & Ward (Jessica Powers)
Templegate Publishers (Franz Jägerstätter)
Wheater/Maryknoll Missioners (Teresa of Calcutta, Oscar Romero)
Gethsemani Abbey (Thomas Merton)
Ateliers et Presses de Taizé (Roger of Taizé)
Franciscan Sisters of Perpetual Adoration (Thea Bowman)

1   2   3   4   5   6   7   8   9

Library of Congress Cataloging-in-Publication Data

Zagano, Phyllis.
    Twentieth-century apostles : contemporary spirituality in action / Phyllis Zagano.
        p.   cm.
    Includes bibliographical references.
    ISBN 0-8146-2554-1 (alk. paper)
    1. Christian life—Catholic authors.   I. Title.
BX2350.2.Z34   1999
282'.092'2—dc21
    [B]   98-41098
                                                              CIP

Thanks, Mary

Contents

Acknowledgments

CARMEL OF THE MOTHER OF GOD
Poems from *The Lantern Burns* by Jessica Powers. Used by permission of the Carmel of the Mother of God, Pewaukee, Wisconsin.

COMMONWEAL MAGAZINE
"The Scandal of the Works of Mercy" by Dorothy Day. Used by permission of Commonweal Magazine, New York, New York.

FRANCISCAN SISTERS OF PERPETUAL ADORATION
"Cosmic Spirituality: No Neutral Ground" by Thea Bowman, presented at the 1987 Religious Formation Conference. Provided by the Franciscan Sisters of Perpetual Adoration Archives. Used by permission of the Franciscan Sisters of Perpetual Adoration.

HARCOURT BRACE & COMPANY
Excerpt from *Christianity and Evolution* by Pierre Teilhard de Chardin, copyright © 1969 by Editions de Seuil, English translation by Rene Hague copyright © 1971 by William Collins Sons & Company, Ltd. and Harcourt Brace & Company, reprinted by permission of Harcourt Brace & Company.

HARPERCOLLINS PUBLISHERS
Texts from *The Divine Milieu* by Pierre Teilhard de Chardin, © by Editions du Seuil, Paris. English translation copyright © 1960 by Wm. Collins & Sons, Co., London, and Harper & Row, Publishers, Inc., New York. Renewed © 1988 by Harper & Row Publishers, Inc. reprinted by permission of HarperCollins Publishers, Inc.

PRESIDENT AND FELLOWS OF HARVARD COLLEGE
Texts from *From Brokenness to Community* by Jean Vanier. Reprinted with permission from Jean Vanier, *From Brokenness to Community*, 18–19, Paulist Press. The Harold M. Wit Lectures, Harvard Divinity School. Copyright 1992 President and Fellows of Harvard College. All rights reserved.

MARQUETTE UNIVERSITY ARCHIVES
Texts from the unpublished letters of Jessica Powers to Margaret Ellen Traxler, SSND. Used by Permission of the Carmel of the Mother of God, Pewaukee, Wisconsin and Sr. Margaret Ellen Traxler, SSND.

MARYKNOLL MISSION ARCHIVES
Texts from the unpublished letters and documents of Ita Ford, M.M. Used by permission of the Maryknoll Sisters of St. Dominic, Inc.

MERTON LEGACY TRUST
"Contemplation in a World of Action" by Thomas Merton used by permission of the Merton Legacy Trust.

NEW DIRECTIONS
Texts by Thomas Merton from *Seeds of Contemplation*. Copyright © 1961 by Our Lady of Gethsemani Abbey. Reprinted by permission of New Directions Publishing Corp. "We Are One Man" by Thomas Merton from *New Seeds of Contemplation*. Copyright © 1961 by The Abbey of Gethsemani, Inc. Reprinted by permission of New Directions Publishing Corp. "The Annunciation" by Thomas Merton from *The Collected Poems of Thomas Merton*. Copyright © 1948 by New Directions Publishing Corporation, 1977 by The Trustees of the Merton Legacy Trust. Reprinted by Permission of New Directions Publishing Corp.

ORBIS BOOKS
Texts from *Romero: A Life*. Copyright © 1989 by Chicago Province of the Society of Jesus. Used by permission of Orbis Books, Maryknoll, New York.

PAULIST PRESS
Texts from *Community and Growth* by Jean Vanier © translation 1979 by Jean Vanier 2nd revised edition © 1989 Jean Vanier. Used by permission of Paulist Press.

Texts from *Followers of Jesus* by Jean Vanier © 1973. The Scripture quotations are from the Revised Standard Version Common Bible. Used by permission of Paulist Press.

LAURENCE POLLINGER LIMITED
Selection from "We Are One Man" from *New Seeds of Contemplation,* and "The Annunciation" from *The Collected Poems of Thomas Merton*. Reprinted with permission of Laurence Pollinger Limited, United Kingdom executors of Thomas Merton.

SHEED AND WARD
Poems from *Selected Poetry of Jessica Powers,* edited by Regina Siegfried and Robert Morneau. Copyright © 1989 by Sheed and Ward. Reprinted with the permission of Sheed and Ward, 115 E. Armour Blvd., Kansas City, Missouri 64111.

TAIZÉ COMMUNITY
From *No Greater Love: Sources of Taizé* by Brother Roger. Originally published as *Amour de tout amour* © Ateliers et Presses de Taizé 1990, Translation © Ateliers et Presses de Taizé 1991. Reprinted by permission of the Taizé Community.

TEMPLEGATE PUBLISHERS
Texts from *In Solitary Witness* by Gordon Zahn Copyright © 1964, 1986 by Gordon C. Zahn. Published by Templegate Publishers, Springfield, Illinois. Used with permission.

Preface

This book has been a delightfully collegial enterprise, and so I applaud all who had a hand in it.

I am grateful to the many friends and colleagues who helped me develop the representative list of twelve, including and especially Kathryn King, F.S.P., Maire McQuillan, R.S.H.M. and Terrence W. Tilley; the librarians who helped me search out the twelve, at Boston University: Raymond Van De Moortell and James Gallagher, at Marymount College: Jo Ellen Morrison and M. St. Edward McLaughlin, R.S.H.M.; my student assistants, Lenin Martell at Boston University and Tamika Davis at Marymount; and Kenneth Holmes at Boston University, who made the administrative tasks of this work so much easier.

I thank as well the archivists and others who helped me search for documents, including the Carmelite Sisters of Pewaukee, Wisconsin; Jolyce Greteman, F.S.P.A., of the Franciscan Sisters of Perpetual Adoration Archives; Ellen Pierce of the Maryknoll Archives; Philip Runkel of the Marquette University Archives.

My deep thanks go as well to members of my family and my friends who encouraged me as I struck out on this new path in June, 1997.

The book is dedicated, with thanks, to Mary Milligan, R.S.H.M., who years ago explained the meaning of not a few words to me, especially "apostle" and "zeal."

March 19, 1998
New York, New York

Introduction

Who is an apostle?

We know the Twelve from scripture: "Simon who is known as Peter, and his brother Andrew; James the son of Zebedee, and his brother John; Philip and Bartholomew; Thomas, and Matthew the tax collector; James the son of Alphaeus, and Thaddeus; Simon the Zealot, and Judas Iscariot, who was also his betrayer. These twelve Jesus sent out . . ." (Matt 10:2-5) Then there were eleven, until Matthias was chosen to replace Judas.

Apostle. Its Greek root is mission-oriented, and means "to send forth." In ancient literature, the "sending forth" most often was a naval expedition; in Scripture "apostle" occasionally gathers in others along with the Twelve. While the New Testament seems only to call the Twelve plus Paul (particularly in Luke) "apostles," many passages expand the meaning a little.

It is that usage I intend. There are many who, like Paul, never received their commissions directly from Jesus in the flesh, but who surely were both called and sent by the living Jesus in their souls. Like Paul, they never expressly claimed to be apostles, but their implicit right to be known as such is based on their living the common characteristics of an apostle: personal election by Jesus, and personal experience of the living Jesus, in life (as with the Twelve) or in the resurrection (as with Paul). Called and sent, they proclaim the risen Lord. They carry on the tradition. They are the basic constitutive elements of the Church.

So with the twelve twentieth-century apostles who follow in these pages. The inheritance of the apostolic office to this day does not restrict the inheritance of the apostolate;

the exercise of the apostolic mission is not limited to popes and bishops. The characteristically apostle-like response of these twelve to being both called and sent by Jesus, intimately, personally, continually, has been lived by thousands of other men and women through the centuries. Their responses in zeal to the call both to be holy and to encourage the holiness of others identify them with the characteristic generosity of the apostle. Their apostolic mission, combined with their ministry, is clear in its definition and inseparable from their lives of prayer.

Each of these twentieth-century apostles lives the essential characteristics of the apostle that I sought: personal identification with Jesus Christ and a sharing of his love for the Father, and for all humanity, with an intensity that necessarily spills over to a deep desire to move others to share those identical loves. Their lives are lighted by the flame of zeal, and everything is illuminated by this flame: their lives are lived for the love of God and the good of souls.

The twelve gathered here present themselves as possessors of that zeal. Of course others can make other lists. I selected apostles of this century whose lives and writings bespoke both their deep relationships with God and their intense involvement with the world around them. I tried to span the century, to find men and women of various descriptions who possessed the common attributes of the apostle.

These are attributes that grow with the gift of grace, but I believe any Christian has the capacity for the singular self-donation that would eventuate in our recognizing him or her as an apostle. So these lives and their writings are presented with the hope that they will encourage others to live similarly.

It is their encouragement that is so very important. More than anything, I wanted to answer the critics and naysayers who surround both us and them, who attempt to crowd into minds and hearts chirping that only this or another attitude or way of life bespeaks the apostolate, only this or another attitude displays the spirit of zeal in one's life. If all are called to be apostles, and the singular characteristic of an apostle is zeal, there is clearly nothing more crushing to any Christian than to say he or she is without zeal. Yet insecure and judgmental people do that every day in one way or another.

They should be ignored, because the principal Enemy of the apostle is in ranks with them, arguing with perfect logic that prayer should be abandoned, the mission ought not be taken up, the ministry should be let go, and the community should be forgotten. They serve the Enemy in presenting doubt disguised as their own zeal, not for the saving of souls (their own or others) but for the saving of position, reputation, comfort and ease. They are unable to take chances.

Real apostles take chances. Each of the twentieth century apostles who follows fought the various guises of the Enemy, in the flesh and in the mind, and each has succeeded in abandoning the self-doubt so cruelly sown and nurtured by others. All of these apostles have served the Gospel through the service of their worlds, in the giving of their talents and enterprising natures over to the people of God, who even today search and hope for more apostles to take their places. The lives of these apostles span this century, as historical records of our progress and as predictors of times to come. Called and sent, they lead us all in lives of prayer and service.

Charles de Foucauld (1858–1916) seems the wandering failure. He began his adult life as a *bon vivant,* a French military officer, a world traveler. He abandoned the life of an explorer to become a Trappist, but left the order shortly before his ordination to serve the simple in the lowest of positions, becoming a gatekeeper and handyman for a Poor Clare monastery. The prioress urged him to give away his solitude and to accept orders, which he did, working his entire life as a missionary in the sub-Sahara, until his death at the hands of rebels.

Teilhard de Chardin (1881–1955), a French Jesuit, was not permitted to publish his spiritual theology during his life, although his work as a paleontologist was well regarded. His "metaphysic of evolution" held that the human species was moving toward a cosmic spiritual oneness in the person of Christ. In the years following his death in New York, on Easter Sunday 1955, this vision touched the world, and it continues to do so.

Giovanni Battista Montini (Paul VI) (1897–1978) is the first modern pope, the first to travel to the New World. His papacy began with Vatican II and ended with his lying in a simple pine coffin in the center of St. Peter's Square. He lived a life of singular erudition with unwavering dedication to the management of the Church and its tasks. He is remembered for his stance on birth control in *Humanae vitae,* for widespread liturgical reform, and for *Inter insigniores,* the 1976 document arguing against the ordination of women.

Dorothy Day (1897–1980) began her life as an unlikely apostle, drawn as she was to radical socialism and the political issues of the day. A mid-westerner turned New Yorker, she worked as a writer and editor on various magazines, living for a while a bohemian life. Her radicality was transformed by the Gospel to an apostolate of caring for the poor. She is remembered for *The Catholic Worker* newspaper and Houses of Hospitality.

Jessica Powers (1905–1988), poet and prioress, spent her life in Wisconsin Carmels, but her poetry reflects the constant movement and constant change that bespeaks the apostolic life. There is of course her cloistered solitude, but within and without that in time and in space she is ever in transition, ever moving to another level of contact with the Lord and the resurrection of the human family.

Franz Jägerstätter (1907–1943) was an Austrian church sacristan beheaded in Berlin for failing to report to military service under Hitler. The sacrifice of this married father of three was born of his absolute opposition to the Third Reich, and his witness is not wholly understood even today. Despite that, his simple home has become a place of pilgrimage, and the Church has opened his beatification process.

Teresa of Calcutta (1910–1997) moved from plain beginnings in Skopje, Macedonia, to international renown as a lover of the abandoned and dying poor. The order she founded in 1950 in India, the Missionaries of Charity, serve the poorest of the poor in over twenty-five countries of the world, living her own recognition that "Today it is very fashionable to talk about the poor. Unfortunately, it is not fashionable to talk with them."

Thomas Merton (1915–1968) was a Trappist monk of the Abbey of Gethsemani, Kentucky, from 1941 to 1968. His life began in Prades, France, and ended with his accidental death near Bangkok, Thailand. His twenty-seven years as monk and writer are marked by scores of poems, magazine articles, essays, pamphlets, translations, journals, letters, and not a few books, each pointing to the engagement of the soul with the living realities of God, self, and others.

Roger of Taizé (1915–), born Roger Louis Schutz-Marsauche in Switzerland, began solitary monastic life in a small French village of Taizé, mid-way between Cluny and Citeaux, in 1939. Ten years later the first seven of his brothers pronounced permanent vows with Brother Roger as prior. Since then Taizé, an ecumenical monastic community of men, has grown to worldwide proportions, with brothers living at Taizé and in small groups among the poor around the world.

Oscar Romero (1917–1980) was born and died in El Salvador, martyred as he said Mass on March 24, 1980. His short term as archbishop of San Salvador saw him radicalized to side with the poor in his tiny fractured nation. His radio homilies and constant public presence argued for human liberation as a gospel right of all. He spoke for the poor and stood with and for the Church persecuted. The Church of El Salvador has asked that he be named a saint.

Jean Vanier (1928–), a Canadian, has lived for over thirty years in one or another of the houses of L'Arche, which he founded for mentally handicapped men in Trosly-Breuil, near Compiegne in the north of France. His work is his message: the dignity of the human person requires that each be treated with respect. His alternative to institutionalization for the handicapped forms a powerful Gospel argument for the sanctity of all life.

Thea Bowman (1937–1990) entered life in Yazoo City, Mississippi, and left it not too far away at age fifty-two, after a six-year struggle with breast cancer and an adult life that centered on her African-American Catholic identity. She was irrepressibly joyful and unassailably sensible; she sang and spoke the wisdom of her elders and challenged the rest of the Church to sing along with her.

Each of these men and women lived in an extraordinary century that saw both expanded and collapsed horizons through technology and travel. Those to whom these apostles ministered witnessed greater and deeper political, economic, and social repression made possible by scientific "advances" and cultural "shifts." Ironically, the very mechanisms that made possible various repressions concurrently improved opportunities for their apostolic works. Teilhard de Chardin's scientific discoveries nurtured his spirituality; Oscar Romero used radio to oppose the systemic evil of El Salvador; Paul VI traveled by jet to speak at the United Nations; Brother Roger invites the young to travel to Taizé with a Web page; Thea Bowman lives in videotapes and recordings of her preaching. The technologies that may have increased suffering in the world also increased their abilities to alleviate it.

The mark of their ongoing commitment was their zeal: their burning desire for their own holiness and the holiness of others, and their tireless application of time and talent to the specific problems of the day, whether it be Dorothy Day arguing against war and on behalf of the poor, or Jessica Powers writing of the constant interior struggle in identifying with the living Christ, or Franz Jägerstätter's clarity of thought in the midst of the Third Reich. Their lives of zeal, lived in the desert, as with Charles de Foucauld, or in the monastery, as with Thomas Merton, set markers for all who learn about them. We can each be inspired by the consummate commitment of Jean Vanier, and of Mother Teresa, even if replication of their specific accomplishments seems unattainable.

Each of these modern apostles took risks, both physical and intellectual. Most were excoriated by friends and foes alike; two died martyrs. Their witness to the possibilities of the resurrection in the lives of all whom they met spilled into everything they did and said. Tomorrow more will be called to join them, but today we call them "apostles" and know that they lived dedicated lives of love that explain to all the true meaning of the word and notion "zeal."

Charles de Foucauld
1858–1916

Charles de Foucauld was born to a noble family in Strasbourg, France on September 15, 1858, and was a penniless missionary when killed by rebels in Tamanrasset, Algeria, on December 1, 1916.

By the time he was six years old his parents were dead; he was raised by his maternal grandfather Colonel Charles de Morlet. The 1870 war drove his family from Strasbourg to Nancy, where he was educated until he entered St. Cyr, the French military academy, in 1876 at age eighteen. His beloved grandfather died the following year, and his grief transformed to a combination of depression and dissoluteness: he wasted the funds he inherited. Charles completed his military education at the Cavalry School at Saumur, and from age twenty to twenty-four he served as an officer in the French army. He resigned in 1882 to explore the closed and secret territory of Morocco on his own, disguised as a rabbi from Central Europe and with the assistance of a true rabbi as his guide. His expedition was both dangerous and successful, and the French Geographical Society awarded him its gold medal.

His journey to the interior of North Africa began the journey to his own interior as well. As the new century beckoned, the gay Charles de Foucauld, a baptized and confirmed (albeit lapsed) Catholic, reflected on the lives of those whom he met in Africa and those whom he found on his return to Paris: "I found myself with people who were very intelligent, virtuous and Christian. I told myself that perhaps this religion is not so absurd after all. At the same time, I felt a very strong interior grace. I started to go into Church, even though I didn't believe. Only there did I feel at ease, I spent long hours repeating that strange prayer, 'God if you do exist, make me know you.'"

Not long thereafter he experienced a deep interior conversion, confessing himself to the well-known spiritual director Fr. Henry Huvelin, who soon advised him to travel on a pilgrimage to the Holy Land. Here Charles met the face of Jesus, realizing that at Nazareth Christ lived for thirty years as a simple tradesman. He later recalled in a letter to his friend Henry de Castrie "My religious vocation came at the same time as my faith. . . . I did not feel that I was to imitate His public life of preaching; I ought then to imitate the hidden life of the poor, humble workman of Nazareth."

First he went to the Trappists. In January 1890 Charles de Foucauld entered the Trappist Monastery of Notre Dame des Neiges in France, to be transferred six months later for his novitiate to the Trappist Monastery of Akbes in Syria. He left the Trappists after seven years to further pursue his dream of the hidden life at Nazareth, where he became a servant and simple workman for the Poor Clare Monastery. After much encouragement from the Poor Clare Abbess Mère St. Michael, Charles was ordained a priest in 1901. Within a few months he was in Algeria as a poor missionary, seeking to befriend all comers, no matter their religious beliefs, striving always to imitate the humble Jesus and so teach the kindness of his poor master through his own kindness and poverty.

He traveled to the Sahara, to Beni-Abbes near the Moroccan frontier to live "the hidden life of Jesus" as a true hermit. He lived as a solitary, concentrating on prayer and adoration of Christ present in the Sacrament, but he became a friend to all as well. He was especially distressed at the conditions of slavery that existed within and without Africa, and he constantly decried the essential injustice of its very existence to all his influential friends.

The Sahara in the earliest part of this century was a place of warring factions and tribal rivalries. No priest had gone before to the south of Beni-Abbes, to the Touareg country in the Haggar. He found another call to pick up and go, this time in early 1904. A ten-month journey of nearly three thousand miles brought him to the southern part of Algeria, to a place called Tamanrasset. There he was accepted by the chief of the Haggar, Moussa Ag Amastane. He learned the Touareg language (Tamahaq), and began a French-Touareg dictionary, and a Touareg New Testament. He created a fraternity in the Haggar, a collection of four huts that withstood with him the famine of 1906–1907, when his friends traveled long distances to obtain the goat's milk that saved his life. He was about to turn fifty, and his friendships deepened as he became truly interdependent with the community about him.

Despite his fairly constant efforts, he never established a religious family during his life time. He three times returned to France to see his family and to attempt to establish a lay fraternity that would have as its apostolic goal missionary work with non-Christians.

Charles de Foucauld lived for ten fairly peaceful years in the Haggar, but the edges of World War I brought him martyrdom at the hands of rebels, whom he did not resist. He was shot in the head and discovered buried in a common grave with three others five days later. His re-interred body was removed to Al-Golea in 1929; his heart remains buried at Tamanrasset.

From Letters of Charles de Foucauld[1]

October 9, 1907. To Mme. de Bondy

By the last post I wrote at length to the abbé Huvelin, telling him what I have already told you, and in more detail. Seeing that it is not possible in a Trappist monastery to lead the life of poverty, abjection, effective detachment, humility, and even recollection, of our Lord at Nazareth, I have to ask myself if He implanted these burning desires in me simply in order that I might sacrifice them or if, since no congregation in the Church to-day provides the possibility of leading with our Lord the life that He led on earth, it is indicated that I should look for a few souls with whom could be made the beginning of a small congregation of another kind. Its object would be to imitate our Lord's life as exactly as possible, living solely by manual work, without begging or accepting even unsolicited alms, following the counsels of perfection to the letter—possessing nothing, giving to whomsoever who asks, asking for nothing in return, going without as much as possible, in the first place in order to become more and more like Jesus Christ and then, almost as much, to give all possible to Him in the person of the poor. To work would be added much prayer, but no choir office, for this is an obstacle to strangers and is little help towards the sanctification of the uneducated. The religious would form only small groups, little dove-cots like Carmels; large monasteries almost necessarily take on a material importance that is a foe of humble obscurity: these groups could be established everywhere, but especially in heathen lands, where it would be such happiness to increase the love and servants of our Lord Jesus.

That is what I have been thinking for about two months. I had the first idea after the winter regular visitation, but it developed only very slowly; then, when I had studied our new constitutions, two months and a half ago, ideas became much more frequent and took a more striking form; finally the matter became so insistent that about three weeks ago I felt bound to speak of it to my confessor, Father Polycarp, asking him if these thoughts came from God, from the Devil, or from my imagination. He told me to put them from my mind for the present and to await such time as God should provide—as He would if the idea was from Him. This seemed very wise advice, and I acted accordingly. I put my own wishes into the hands of God, asking Him to allow me to think only those things that are for His greater glory.

April 10, 1907. To Mme. de Bondy

A week ago I was sent to pray beside a poor Syrian workman who died in the neighbouring hamlet. What a difference between his house and our dwelling-place!—*I long for Nazareth.*

June 18, 1907. To Raymund de Blic

It is a happiness of the country to be able to have all whom one loves around one . . . and it is a very great happiness. In that case, you will say, why have you taken yourself off so far?

Because I am not looking for joy but am drawn after the 'fragrance of His perfumes', that Jesus who loves us so much . . . and if I have found delight in following Him it is without having looked for it. And that delight does not prevent me from feeling deeply the sadness of being separated from those whom I love.

July 22, 1907. To Mme. de Bondy

Like the doorkeeper in a monastery I am interrupted from time to time by knocking at the door: it is the poor, besides whom I have scarcely any other visitors at present. All those who are able are now anything up to 500 miles from here, in places that have had rain: the poor, having no camels to carry them, are held on a short tether. God has done me a great grace: there has been a military reorganization in the extreme south of Algeria and hence-forward my friend Laperrine will be stationed at In-Salah, with Uargla, Al-Golea, and all the Tuaregs of the Hoggar, the Asjer and the Taitok within his command.

January 15, 1908. To Mme. de Bondy

In fulfilment of my promise always to tell you the truth I must say that for a fortnight past I have been rather tired—not ill, but weak, without appetite, and sleeping badly. It is simply and solely due to too much work and cutting down my hours for sleep. The rather sharp cold, to which I am sensitive, has made it worse: for several days I have been blowing like a broken-winded old horse, but with no pain or being unwell enough to stop work. I think the remedy lies in more sleep and more strengthening food, and then the first days of spring will do the rest; so I have written a letter to Henry Laperrine that is a disgrace to a hermit—asking him to sent me some condensed milk, a little wine (!) and other similar things.

June 4, 1908. To Mme. de Bondy

To convert this country you want priests and nuns and lay people who will get into contact with the Mohammedans, drawing them imperceptibly, educating and civilizing them till they are men and women out of whom Christians can be made. You cannot here make them Christians first and civilize them afterwards: the only possible way is the other, and much slower, one of first educating and civilizing and then converting. But that requires a very big effort. One can be patient for centuries or till the end of the world when it is only a question of building churches of stone, but there must be no delay when it is a matter of saving human souls in danger.

September 20, 1908. To Mme. de Bondy

I am well, but I feel myself getting old: I work more and more slowly, like a tired man—I am just fifty, and feel it. All the more do I wish that there were others available to step into my place when I have gone altogether: I enjoy solitude for myself—but how many things I could do were I not alone! It is sad to see souls endangered and Christ's kingdom restricted for want of workers: if workers were only *willing to come forward* they could do so much good here and now. I am ashamed at how little is done by our country: not that she does nothing, but it is so much less than it might and ought to be. I don't know but that I shall finish by going to Algiers to talk with the superior general of the White Fathers about it, and perhaps to Paris to talk with the abbé Huvelin. Something must be done—these people can't be left without priests for ever. I should like to take a favourable specimen of the Tuaregs with me to France. M. Huvelin will tell me whether all this is God's will or simply temptation and delusion.

December 1, 1916. To Mme. de Bondy

Your sufferings, the worrying uncertainties in the past and more recently, received with good will and offered to God in union with and for the intentions of the sufferings of Jesus, these are not the only thing, but they are the most valuable that God gives to you in order that you may come before Him with full hands. Self-abnegation is the best of all ways of uniting oneself with Jesus and of bringing good to others: as St John-of-the-Cross keeps on saying, 'To suffer and to love is the greatest thing that can be done in this world. We know when we suffer, we do not always know when we love, and that is one suffering the more; but we can will to love, and to will it is to do it'. We think that we do not love enough, and that is true, for one can never love enough; but God, who knows of what clay we are made, who loves us far more than any mother is able to love her child, who never dies, God has told us that He will not spurn those who come to Him. . . .

It does not seem to me that at present there is any danger to us from Tripolitania and the Senussi; our troops are strongly reinforced and I hope that they will be able to force the enemy back beyond our frontier. There have been no alarms since September and the country is very quiet.

Prayer of Abandonment of Brother Charles of Jesus

Father,
I abandon myself into your hands;
do with me what you will.
Whatever you may do, I will always thank you:
I am ready for all, I accept all.
Let only your will be done in me,
and in all your creatures;
No more do I wish than this, O Lord.

Into your hands I commend my soul
I offer it to you with all the Love of my heart,
for I love you, Lord, and so need to give myself,
to surrender myself into your hands without reserve,
and with boundless confidence,
for you are my Father.

Teilhard de Chardin
1881–1955

Pierre Teilhard de Chardin was a French Jesuit priest, pale-ontologist, and philosopher whose work coalesced to the single notion that the human species is evolving, mentally and socially, toward a final spiritual unity.

Born in France, he entered the Society of Jesus at age eighteen and earned a doctorate in paleontology from the Sorbonne at twenty-two. Two years later he was sent to teach at the Jesuit college in Cairo and, except for service as a stretcher bearer in World War I, he spent the rest of his life in geological and paleontological expeditions and research around the world, first to China, where he participated in the discovery of the Peking man (1929), to the Gobi Desert, India, Kashmir, Java and Burma. He spent the World War II years 1939–1945 in Peking, unable to leave because of the war. He then moved to New York, from which base at the Wenner-Gren Foundation he made two paleontological and archeological expeditions to South Africa.

Teilhard's scientific writings and achievements are con-siderable and well noted by the scientists of his time, and predominantly focus on mammalian paleontology. His philo-sophical and theological writings, however, were neither well known nor published during his life. He composed his two major philosophical works, *The Divine Milieu* (1957) and *The Phenomenon of Man* (1955), in the 1920s and 1930s, but his Jesuit superiors forbade him permission to publish. Collections of his philosophical essays followed his death in rapid succession: *The Appearance of Man* (1956), *The Vision of the Past* (1957), and *Science and Christ* (1965). Multiple vol-umes of letters and other writings have appeared since then.

His total vision comprised what has been called a metaphysic of evolution, which held that evolution was a process converging to a final unity, the Omega point. This marks both personal and corporate authenticity: participation in an evolution that encompasses all and converges in the person of Christ. The appearance of man made this possible, for man is the only sentient and reflective being: humans know, and they know that they know. Teilhard reasoned that human physical evolution was complete; human social evolution would progress, through technology, communications, and urbanization, to enable multiple links between and among cultures, political structures and economies in geometric progression.

The culmination of this social evolution would be a convergence between humanity and its material world and the supernatural order, initiated by the Second Coming of Christ. What Teilhard reasoned, and what was so strikingly challenging to his contemporaries, was his emphasis on the argument that the reason Christ existed was to lead the material world and humanity to this cosmic redemption, not to conquer evil, which was merely the byproduct of the forward evolution he envisioned.

His transformation of the God of the Gospel to the God of Evolution was not well met by some critics. His posthumous publications brought him great notoriety, and earned his readers a warning from the Holy Office against the uncritical acceptance of his ideas. Others, however, found his reasoning strikingly consonant with the contemplative notion that all things conspire and converge to the good. In a 1961 letter to Margaret Ellen Traxler, S.N.D., Jessica Powers wrote: "Recently I had an opportunity to read *The Divine Milieu*. Even if it should not be all truth, as some theologians claim, it opens up vistas. One cannot help but feel that we are hurrying toward some tremendous fulfillment when God will be All in all. Even now it is breathtaking (if one stops to consider) that we are living in a divine milieu. Everything becomes wonderful, beyond words to express that wonder."[1]

His theories applied in personal terms are summarized in his essay "The Mystical Milieu," which places the person at the center of five conjoined circles: presence (love of creation), consistence, (recognition of God in all), energy (participation in God's action), spirit (recognition of the goal of freedom), and person (cosmic communion in Christ). Each circle explains the others, and his progression shows the influence of the Exercises of St. Ignatius of Loyola on his life and thought.

Pierre Teilhard de Chardin died on Easter Sunday, 1955, in New York.

From *Christianity and Evolution*[2]

The Gospel Message

"There has been too much talk of lambs. Give the lions a chance." Too much gentleness and not enough force. Those symbols are a fair summary of my feelings and my theme, as I turn to the question of readjusting the gospel teaching to the modern world.

This question is vital. The great majority of our contemporaries have no distinct interest in the meaning to be attached to the mysteries of the Incarnation and the Redemption. All, however, react sharply to the interior effects of agreement or disagreement which they produce for them in the field of morality and mysticism. We Christians often flatter ourselves that if so many Gentiles still fight shy of the Faith it is because the ideal we hold up for their admiration is too perfect and too difficult. This is an illusion. A noble difficulty has always fascinated souls. The truth about today's gospel is that it has ceased, or practically ceased, to have any attraction because it has become *unintelligible*. In a world which has been so awesomely modified, the same words are being repeated to us as served our fathers. *A priori*, it would be a safe bet that these antique expressions can no longer satisfy us.* In fact, the best non-believers I know would feel that they were falling short of

---

* Unless interpreted in the light of the present dimensions of the world.

their moral ideal if they went through the gesture of conversion: they have told me so themselves.

Here again, if we are to remain faithful to the gospel, we have to adjust its spiritual code to the new shape of the universe. Henceforth the universe assumes an additional dimension for our experience. It has ceased to be the formal garden from which we are temporarily banished by a whim of the Creator. It has become the great work in process of completion which we have to save by saving ourselves. We are finding out that we are the elements responsible, at the atomic level, for a cosmogenesis. Transferred into this new space, what becomes of Christian moral rules of conduct? How are they to accommodate themselves if they are still to remain themselves?

One sentence will serve as an answer: By becoming, for God, the reinforcement of evolution. Hitherto the Christian was brought up under the impression that he could attain God only by abandoning everything. He is now discovering that he cannot be saved except through the universe and as a continuation of the universe. There was a time when the gospel teaching could be summed up in the words of the Epistle: *"Religio munda haec est: visitare pupillos et viduas, et immaculatum se custodire ab hoc saeculo."** That time is gone for ever; or rather, the words of St James must be interpreted with the full moral depth that new horizons enable us to see in them.

To worship was formerly to prefer God to things, relating them to him and sacrificing them for him. To worship is now becoming to devote oneself body and soul to the creative act, associating oneself with that act in order to fulfil the world by hard work and intellectual exploration.

To love one's neighbour was formerly to do him no injury and to bind up his wounds. Henceforth charity, without losing any of its compassion, will attain its full meaning in life given for common progress.

To be pure was formerly to hold oneself aloof from, to guard against, contamination. The name of chastity will be given tomorrow primarily to sublimation of the powers of the flesh and of all passion.

---

* "Religion that is pure and undefiled . . . is this: to visit orphans and widows . . . and to keep oneself unstained from the world" (James 1:27).

To be detached was formerly to attach no value to things, and to abstain from them, as far as possible. To be detached will become more and more to leave behind every truth and every beauty in turn, precisely in virtue of the love one has for them.

To be resigned could formerly mean passive acceptance of present conditions in the universe. Resignation will now be confined to the wrestler capitulating in the grip of the angel.

It used to appear that there were only two attitudes mathematically possible for man: to love heaven or to love earth. With a new view of space, a third road is opening up: to make our way to heaven *through* earth. There is a communion (the true communion) with God through the world; and to surrender oneself to it is not to take the impossible step of trying to serve two masters.

Such a Christianity is still in reality the true gospel teaching, since it represents the same force applied to the elevation of mankind above the tangible, in a common love.

Yet, at the same time, this teaching has no taint of the opium which we are accused with such bitterness (and not without justification) of dispensing to the masses.

It is no longer, even simply the soothing oil poured into the wounds of mankind, the lubrication for its labouring mechanism.

The truth is that it comes to us as the animator of human action, to which it offers the clear-cut ideal of a divine figure, discernible in history, in which all that is essentially most precious in the universe is concentrated and preserved.

It provides the exact answer to all the doubts and aspirations of an age suddenly woken into consciousness of its future.

This presentation of the gospel, and this alone, so far as we can judge, stands out as capable of justifying and maintaining in the world the fundamental zest for life.

It is the very religion of evolution.

Conclusion

Some years ago, in the course of a conversation with an old missionary—something of a visionary, but universally regarded as a saint—I heard him make the following surprising statement: "History shows that no religion has been able to maintain itself in the world for more than two thousand years. Once that time has run out, they all die. And it is coming up to two thousand years for Christianity . . ." By that he, as a prophet, meant that the end of the world was close at hand; but to me his words had a graver import.

Two thousand years, more or less, is indeed a long stage for man particularly if, as is happening today, there has just been added to it the critical point of a "change of age." So many attitudes and outlooks are modified after twenty centuries that, in the context of religion, we have to slough off the old skin. Our formulas have become narrow and inflexible; we find them irksome, and they have ceased to have an emotional impact on us. There must be a "moult" if we are to continue to live.

As a Christian, I am barred from believing that it is possible for Christianity to disappear in this period of transition that is upon us, as has happened to other religions. I believe Christianity to be immortal. But this immortality of our faith does not prevent it from being subject (even as it rises above them) to the general laws of periodicity which govern all life. I recognize, accordingly, that at the present moment Christianity (exactly like the mankind it embraces) is reaching the end of one of the natural cycles of its existence.

By dint of repeating and developing in the abstract the expression of our dogmas, we are well on the way to losing ourselves in the clouds where neither the turmoil nor the aspirations nor the living vigour of the earth can penetrate. Religiously, we are living, in relation to the world, in a twofold intellectual and emotional isolation: an indication that the time for a renewal is close at hand. After what will soon be two thousand years, Christ must be born again, he must be reincarnated in a world that has become too different from that in which he lived. Christ cannot reappear tangibly among us; but he can reveal to our minds a new and triumphant aspect of his former countenance.

I believe that the Messiah whom we await, whom we all without any doubt await, is the universal Christ; that is to say, the Christ of evolution.

Unpublished, Tientsin, Christmas 1933. Printed from a copy bearing a manuscript note "Revised and corrected" following by the signature "Teilhard."

From *The Divine Milieu*³

Part One: The Divinisation of Our Activities*

Of the two halves or components into which our lives may be divided, the most important, judging by appearances and by the price we set upon it, is the sphere of activity, endeavour and development. There can, of course, be no action without reaction. And, of course, there is nothing in us which in origin and at its deepest is not, as St. Augustine said, *"in nobis, sine nobis."* When we act, as it seems, with the greatest spontaneity and vigour, we are to some extent led by the things we imagine we are controlling. Moreover, the very expansion of our energy (which reveals the core of our autonomous personality) is, ultimately, only our obedience to the will to be and to grow, of which we can master neither the variations of intensity nor the countless forms. We shall return, at the beginning of Part Two, to these essentially passive elements, some of which form part of the vary marrow of our substance, while others are diffused among the interplay of universal causes which we call our "character," our "nature" or our "good and bad luck." For the moment let us consider our life in terms of the categories and definitions which are the most immediate and universal. Everyone can distinguish quiet clearly between the moments in which he is acting and those in which he is acted upon. Let us look at ourselves in one of those phases of dominant activity and try to see how, with the help of our activity and by developing it to the full, the divine presses in upon us and seeks to enter our lives.

1. The Undoubted Existence of the Fact and the Difficulty of Explaining It. The Christian Problem of the Sanctification of Action

Nothing is more certain, dogmatically, than that human action can be sanctified. "Whatever you do," says St. Paul, "do it in the

---

* *Note.* It is of the utmost importance at this point to bear in mind what was said at the end of the Preface. We use the word 'activity' in the ordinary, current sense, without in any way denying—far from it—all that occurs between grace and the will in the infra-experimental spheres of the soul. To repeat: what is most divine in God is that, in an absolute sense, we are nothing apart from Him. The least admixture of what may be called Pelagianism would suffice to ruin immediately the beauties of the divine milieu in the eyes of the "seer."

name of Our Lord Jesus Christ." And the dearest of Christian traditions has always been to interpret those words to mean: in intimate union with Our Lord Jesus Christ. St. Paul himself, after calling upon us to "put on Christ," goes on to forge the famous series of words *collaborare, compati, commori, con-resuscitare,* giving them the fullest possible meaning, a literal meaning even, and expressing the conviction that every human life must—in some sort—become a life in common with the life of Christ. The actions of life, of which we are speaking here, should not, as everyone knows, be understood solely in the sense of religious and devotional works (prayers, fasting, almsgiving). It is the whole of human life, down to its most "natural" zones, which, the Church teaches, can be sanctified. "Whether you eat or whether you drink," St. Paul says. The whole history of the Church is there to attest it. Taken as a whole, then, from the most solemn declarations or examples of the Pontiffs and Doctors of the Church to the advice humbly given by the priest in confession, the general influence and practice of the Church has always been to dignify, ennoble and transfigure in God the duties inherent to one's station in life, the search for natural truth, and the development of human action.

The fact cannot be denied. But its legitimacy, that is its logical coherence with the whole basis of the Christian spirit, is not immediately apparent. How is it that the perspectives opened up by the Kingdom of God do not, by their very presence, shatter the equilibrium and economy of our activities? How can the man who believes in heaven and the Cross continue to believe seriously in the value of worldly occupations? How can the believer, in the name of everything that is most Christian in him, carry out his human duties to the fullest extent and as wholeheartedly and freely as if he were on the direct road to God? That is what is not altogether clear at first sight; and in fact disturbs more minds than one thinks.

The question might be put in this way:

According to the most sacred articles of his *Credo,* the Christian believes that life here below is continued in a life of which the joy, the suffering, the reality, are quite incommensurable with the present conditions in our universe. This contrast and disproportion are enough, by themselves, to rob us of our taste for the world and our interest in it; but to them must be added a positive doctrine of condemnation or contempt for a fallen and vitiated world. "Perfection consists in detachment; the world about us is vanity and ashes." The believer is constantly reading or hearing these austere words. How can he reconcile them with that other counsel, usually coming from the same master and in any case written in his heart by nature, that he must be an example unto the Gentiles in devotion to duty, in energy, and even in leadership in all the spheres opened up by man's activity? There is no need for us to consider the wayward or the lazy who cannot be bothered to acquire knowledge or organise a better life, from which they will benefit a hundred-fold after their last breath, and only contribute to the human task "with the tips of their fingers" (to quote from something once imprudently said). But there is a category of mind (know to every spiritual director) for whom the difficulty takes the form and importance of a constant and paralysing perplexity. Such minds, set upon interior unity, become the victims of a veritable spiritual dualism. On the one hand a very sure instinct, mingled with their love of being and their taste for life, draws them towards the joy of creation and knowledge. On the other hand a higher will to love God above all else makes them afraid of the least division of deflection in their allegiances. In the most spiritual layers of their being they experience a tension between the opposing ebb and flow caused by the attraction of the two rival stars we spoke of at the beginning: God and the world. Which of the two is to made itself more nobly adored?

Depending on the greater or less vitality of the nature of the individual, this conflict is in danger of finding its solution in one of the three following ways: either the Christian will repress his taste for the tangible and force himself to centre his interest on purely religious objects only, trying to live in a world made divine by the exclusion of the largest possible number of worldly objects; or else, harassed by that inward conflict which hampers him, he will dismiss the evangelical counsels and decide to lead what seems to him a complete and human life; or else, again, and this is the most usual case, he will give up any attempt to understand; he will never belong wholly to God, nor ever wholly to things; imperfect in his own eyes, and insincere in the eyes of men, he will become resigned to leading a double life. I am speaking, it should not be forgotten, from experience.

For various reasons, all three of these solutions are dangerous. Whether we become distorted, disgusted or divided, the
result is equally bad, and certainly contrary to that which Christianity should rightly produce in us. There is, without possible
doubt, a fourth way out of the problem: it consists in seeing
how, without making the smallest concession to 'nature' but
with a desire for greater perfection, we can reconcile, and provide mutual nourishment for, the love of God and a healthy love
of the world, a striving towards detachment and a striving towards development.

Let us look at the two solutions that can be brought to the
Christian problem of "the divinisation of human activity," the
first partial, the second complete.

2. An Incomplete Solution: Human Action Has No Value Other Than the Intention Which Directs It

Reduced somewhat crudely and schematically to essentials, the
immediate answer given by spiritual directors to those who ask
them how a Christian who is determined to despise the world
and jealously reserve his heart for God, can love what he is doing
(his work)—in conformity with the Church's teaching that the
faithful should take *not a lesser* but a *fuller* part than the pagan—
may be put thus:

"You are anxious, my friend, to restore the value of your human
endeavour which seems to you to be depreciated by the Christian vision and Christian asceticism. Very well then, pour over
it the marvellous substance of good will. Purify your intention,
and the least of your actions will be filled with God. No doubt
the material side of your actions has no ultimate value. Whether
men discover one truth or one fact more or less, whether or not
they make beautiful music or beautiful pictures, whether their
organisation of the world is more or less successful—all that has
no direct importance for heaven. None of these discoveries or
creations will become one of the stones from which is built the
New Jerusalem. But what will count, up there, what will always
endure, is this: that you have acted in all things *conformably* to
the will of God.

"God obviously has no need of the products of your busy activity, since He could give Himself everything without you. The
only thing that interests Him, the one thing He desires intensely,

is the faithful use of your freedom, and the preference you accord Him over the things around you.

"Try to grasp this: the things which are given to you on earth are given you purely as an exercise, a 'blank sheet' on which you make your own mind and heart. You are on a testing-ground where God can judge whether you are capable of being translated to heaven and into His presence. You are on trial. So that it matters very little what becomes of the fruits of the earth, or what they are worth. The whole question is whether you have used them in order to learn how to obey and how to love.

"You should not, therefore, cling to the coarse outer-covering of human activities: these are but inflammable straw or brittle clay. But try to realise that into each of these humble vessels you can pour, like a sap or a precious liquid, the spirit of obedience and of union with God. If worldly aims have no value in themselves, you can love them for the opportunity they give you of proving your constancy of God."

We are not suggesting that the foregoing words are ever actually used; but we believe they convey a shade of meaning which is often present in spiritual advice, and we are sure that they give a rough idea of what a good number of the 'directed' have understood and retained of the exhortations given them.

On this assumption let us examine the attitude which they recommend.

In the first place this attitude contains an enormous part of truth. It rightly exalts the initial and basic role or intention which is really (as we shall have occasion to repeat) the golden key by which the inward world is opened to the divine Presence. It expresses vigorously the substantial value of the divine will which, by virtue of this attitude, becomes for the Christian (as it was for his divine Model) the life-giving marrow of all earthly nourishment. It reveals a sort or unique milieu, unchanging beneath the diversity and plurality of human works, in which we can settle without ever having to leave it.

These various features are a primary and essential approximation to the solution we are looking for; and we shall certainly retain them in their entirety in the more satisfactory plan of the interior life which will soon be suggested. But they seem to us to lack the fulfilment which our spiritual peace and joy so imperiously demand. The divinisation of our endeavour by the value of the intention put into it infuses a precious soul into all our actions; but *it does not confer the hope of resurrection upon their bodies.* Yet that hope is what we need if our joy is to be complete. It is certainly a very great thing to be able to think that, if we love God, something of our inner activity, of our *operatio,* will never be lost. But will not the work itself of our minds, of our hearts and of our hands—that is to say, our achievements, our products, our *opus*—will not this, too, in some sense be 'eternalised' and saved?

Indeed, Lord, it will be—by virtue of a need which You Yourself have implanted at the very centre of my will! I desire and need that it should be.

I desire it because I love irresistibly all that your continuous help enables me to bring each day to reality. A thought, a material improvement, a harmony, a particular expression of love, the enchanting complexity of a smile or a look, all the new beauties that appear for the first time, in me or around me, on the human face of the earth—I cherish them like children and cannot believe that they will die entirely in the flesh. If I believed that these thing were to wither away for ever, should I have given them life? The more I examine myself, the more I discover this psychological truth: that no one lifts his little finger to do the smallest task unless moved, however obscurely, by the conviction that he is contributing infinitesimally (at least indirectly) to the construction of some absolute—that is to say, to Your work, my God. This may well sound strange or exaggerated to those who act without thoroughly analysing themselves. And yet it is a fundamental law of their action. It requires no less than the attraction of what is called the Absolute, no less than You Yourself, to set in motion the frail liberty with which You have endowed us. And that being so, everything which diminishes my explicit faith in the heavenly value of the results *of my endeavour, lowers irremediably my power to act.*

Show all Your faithful, Lord, in what a full and true sense "their work follows them" into Your Kingdom—opera sequuntur illos. Otherwise they will become like those idle labourers who are not spurred by their task. Or, if human instinct triumphs over their hesitations or the sophisms of a religion upon which not sufficient light has been thrown, they will remain fundamentally divided and frustrated; and it will be said that the sons of heaven cannot compete on the human level, in conviction and hence on equal terms, with the children of the world.

3. The Final Solution: All Endeavour Cooperates to Complete the World 'In Christo Jesu'

The general economy of the salvation (which is to say the divinisation) of our works can be expressed briefly in the following syllogism.

At the heart of our universe, each soul exists for God, in Our Lord.

But all reality, even material reality, around each one of us, exists for our souls.

Hence, all sensible reality, around each one of us, exists, through our souls, for God in Our Lord.

Giovanni Battista Montini
(Paul VI) 1897–1978

Giovanni Battista Montini was sixty-six when his good friend Pope John XXIII died in 1963, a year after the opening of the Second Vatican Council. After his election, Paul VI wrote: "Perhaps the Lord has called me to this service not because I have any aptitude for it, nor so that I can govern the Church in its present difficulties, but so I may suffer something and thus that it may be clear that it is the Lord, and no one else, who guides and saves it."[1]

That the Lord guided his life he was sure, despite its many sufferings. Giovanni Battista Enrico Antonio Maria Montini was born September 26, 1897, at Concesio, in his family's country house not far from Brescia. The middle son of a middle-class family—his father was a politically involved newspaper editor, his mother a Brescia woman educated in a French convent in Milan—Battista early on showed a physical weakness. At sixteen he suffered from heart trouble, and was not expected to live long. Nevertheless, he continued his studies with difficulty and asked to be admitted to the transplanted French Benedictine monastery at Chiari where he often bicycled for Compline. Refused on account of his health by the Benedictines, neither would the Italian army draft him, and he sought a life as secular cleric. The war and the fact that he was the son of a prominent Catholic intellectual allowed the bishop of Brescia to grant him permission to study for the priesthood as a special external student.

As he began his studies there were only five students at the seminary; within a year there were just two. He read widely and deeply beyond his studies, from Mickiewicz's

Book of the Polish Nation to Oscar Wilde's *De Profundis*, and practiced piano in his free time. The war ended and others were studying for priesthood; he was one of fourteen men ordained on May 29, 1920.

But ordained to do what? His physical weakness did not recommend him for anything it seemed, besides more studies. He embarked on ill-fated doctoral studies in history in Rome, then read theology, and eventually obtained an unofficial position with the Secretariat of State in Warsaw. He made friends among the Vatican diplomatic corps and eventually returned to Rome, where he served as papal undersecretary of state and close aide to Pius XII from 1939 to 1954, when he was appointed archbishop of Milan, but not a cardinal, by the pope he so faithfully served. Had he been named cardinal before Pius XII's death he might have been the next pope. As it was, there were curial insiders who opposed the election of Angelo Roncalli, patriarch of Venice, because they feared he would return their exiled Montini to Rome.

Battista was his old friend John XXIII's first cardinal, elevated in 1958. But the new pope left the new Cardinal Montini in Milan, apparently to help move the bishops of Italy toward the concept of the Second Vatican Council. His proximity to power was evident: unlike the majority of the council fathers, during the council Montini lived inside the Vatican. His place in the council was marked early. He celebrated the first Ambrosian Rite Mass ever in St. Peter's, and in the presence of the pope, marking John XXIII's interest in liturgical reform and Cardinal Montini's place in it.

With the old pope dead in 1963, John XXIII's favored successor was elected. Giovanni Battista Montini's election was the fruit of a contested conclave, in which conservative forces tried to stop the prospect of *aggiornamento* begun by John XXIII. Montini chose the name Paul VI. He had been a priest for forty-five years: one in Poland, ten in Milan, and the rest in Rome.

The three things for which the pontificate of Paul VI is best known are liturgical reform, the encyclical *Humanae vitae,* and travel. He was already used to travel; as archbishop of Milan he was to North and South America, and throughout Europe. He guided Vatican II through its final sessions, and personally approved council documents. He guided the liturgical reform of the Church, and traveled widely in the cause of peace and justice. His famous "Jamais la guerre" plea at the United Nations, printed below in its entirety, marked the first time a pope had ever traveled to the United States.

Many efforts at reform were unsuccessful in his papacy. He ignored the results of a Study Commission that said there was absolutely no foundation for refusing to admit women to the lay ministries of lector and acolyte. He allowed the suppression of the mid-1970s study on women deacons by the International Theological Commission. He allowed the Congregation for the Doctrine of the Faith 1976 document *Inter insigniores* denying priestly ordination to women. Still, he named the first two women doctors of the Church, Catherine of Siena and Teresa of Avila.

The world sees him as well as an archconservative on the matter of contraception. No matter the contested versions of how the document came about, *Humanae vitae* opposed artificial contraception under any circumstances and remains criticized—and often ignored—on that count.

His apostolic witness led him to recognize that the keys of Peter were heavy. His ill health led to a deep introspection and intellectual appreciation of the needs of the Church, but his unwavering command of the concept of collegiality led him to seek reconciliation with renegade right-wing Archbishop LeFevre of Switzerland, who refused Vatican II reforms and illicitly trained and ordained priests. Paul VI's own modernization of the papacy leaves him the last crowned pope, and the first to enter into a modern effort toward ecumenism, even as he recognized that the pope himself is perhaps the biggest obstacle in that effort. He died late in the summer of 1978, and was briefly succeeded by John Paul I, then a few months later by John Paul II.

Address of Pope Paul VI to the United Nations
General Assembly, October 4, 1965

As We begin to speak to this audience that is unique in the whole world, We must first of all express Our profound thanks to Mr. Thant, your Secretary General, who was kind enough to invite Us to pay a visit to the United Nations on the occasion of the twentieth anniversary of this world institution for peace and collaboration between the nations of the whole world.

We also want to thank the President of the Assembly, Signor Amintore Fanfani, who has had such kind words for Us from the day on which he took over the office.

We want to thank each of you here present for your kind welcome, and We offer you Our cordial and respectful greetings. Your friendship has brought Us to this gathering and admitted Us to it. It is as a friend that We appear before you.

In addition to Our own respects, We bring you those of the Second Ecumenical Council of the Vatican, now meeting in Rome. The Cardinals who have accompanied Us are its eminent representatives. In their name, as in Our own, We pay honor to all of you and offer you greetings!

This gathering, as you are all well aware, has a twofold nature: it is marked at one and the same time by simplicity and by greatness. By simplicity because the one who is speaking to you is a man like yourselves. He is your brother, and even one of the least among you who represent sovereign states, since he possesses—if you choose to consider Us from this point of view—only a tiny and practically symbolic temporal sovereignty: the minimum needed in order to be free to exercise his spiritual mission and to assure those who deal with him that he is independent of any sovereignty of this world. He has no temporal power, no ambition to enter into competition with you. As a matter of fact, We have nothing to ask, no question to raise; at most a desire to formulate, a permission to seek: that of being allowed to serve you in the area of our competence, with disinterestedness, humility and love.

This is the first declaration that We have to make. As you can see, it is so simple that it may seem insignificant for this assembly, which is used to dealing with extremely important and difficult affairs.

And yet as We were telling you, and you can all sense it, this moment bears the imprint of a unique greatness: it is great for Us, it is great for you.

For Us first of all. You know very well who We are, and whatever your opinion of the Pontiff of Rome maybe you know that Our mission is to bring a message for all mankind. We speak not only in Our own name and in the name of the great Catholic family, but also in the name of the Christian brethren who share in the sentiments We are expressing here, and especially of those who have been kind enough to designate Us explicitly as their spokesman. This is the kind of messenger who, at the end of a long journey, is handing over the letter that has been entrusted to him. Hence We have an awareness of living through a privileged moment—brief though it be—when a wish borne in Our heart for almost twenty centuries is being accomplished. Yes, you recall it. We have been on our way for a long time and We bring a long history with Us. Here We are celebrating the epilogue to a laborious pilgrimage in search of an opportunity to speak heart to heart with the whole world. It began on the day when We were commanded: "Go, bring the good news to all nations!" You are the ones who represent all nations.

Permit Us to say that We have a message, and a happy one, to hand over to each one of you.

1. Our message is meant to be first of all a solemn moral ratification of this lofty Institution, and it comes from Our experience of history. It is as an "expert on mankind" that We bring this Organization the support and approval of Our recent predecessors, that of the Catholic hierarchy and Our own, convinced as We are that this Organization represents the path that has to be taken for modern civilization and for world peace.

In saying this, We are aware that We are speaking for the dead as well as the living: for the dead who have fallen in the terrible wars of the past, dreaming of world peace and harmony; for the living who have survived the wars and who in their hearts condemn in advance those who would try to have them repeated; for other living people too: the younger generation of today who are moving ahead trustfully with every right to expect a better mankind. We also want to speak for the poor, the disinherited, the unfortunate, those who long for justice, a dignified life, liberty, prosperity and progress. People turn to the United Nations as if it were their last hope for peace and harmony. We presume to bring here their tribute of honor and of hope along with Our own. That is why this moment is a great one for you too.

2. We know that you are fully aware of this. So listen now to the rest of Our message, which is directed completely toward the future. This edifice that you have built must never again fall into ruins: it must be improved upon and adapted to the demands which the history of the world will make upon it. You mark a stage in the development of mankind. Henceforth, it is impossible to go back; you must go forward.

You offer the many States which can no longer ignore each other a form of coexistence that is extremely simple and fruitful. First of all, you recognize them and distinguish them from *each other*. Now you certainly do not confer existence on States, but you do qualify each nation as worthy of being seated in the orderly assembly of peoples. You confer recognition of lofty moral and juridical value upon each sovereign national community and you guarantee it an honorable international citizenship. It is in itself a great service to the cause of mankind to define clearly and honor the nations that are the subjects of the world community and to set them up in a juridical position which wins them the recognition and respect of all, and which can serve as the basis for an orderly and stable system of international life. You sanction the great principle that relationships between nations must be regulated by reason, justice, law and negotiation, and not by force, violence, war, nor indeed by fear and deceit.

This is as it should be. And permit Us to congratulate you for having had the wisdom to open up access to this assembly to the young nations, the States that have only recently attained national independence and liberty. Their presence here is proof of the universality and greatheartedness that inspire the principles of this Institution.

This is as it should be. Such is Our praise and Our wish, and as you can see We are not reaching outside to find a basis for them. We are drawing them from within, from the very nature and spirit of your Institution.

3. Your Charter goes ever farther, and Our message moves ahead with it. You are in existence and you are working in order to unite nations, to associate States. Let us use the formula: to

bring them together *with each other*. You are an association, a bridge between peoples, a network of relations between States. We are tempted to say that in a way this characteristic of yours reflects in the temporal order what our Catholic Church intends to be in the spiritual order: one and universal. Nothing loftier can be imagined on the natural level, as far as the ideological structure of mankind is concerned. Your vocation is to bring not just some peoples but all peoples together as brothers. A difficult undertaking? Without a doubt. But this is the nature of your very noble undertaking. Who can fail to see the need and importance of thus gradually coming to the establishment of a world authority capable of taking effective action on the juridical and political planes?

Again We repeat Our wish: go forward! Even more, act in such a way as to bring back into your midst those who have separated themselves from you, and look for means to bring into your pact of brotherhood, honorably and loyally, those who do not yet belong. Act in such a way that those who are still outside will desire and deserve the confidence and trust of everyone, and be generous in according it to them. And you who have the good fortune and honor to sit in this assembly of a peaceful community, listen to Us: so act that this mutual confidence and trust that unites you and allows you to do great and good things may never be stained and never betrayed.

4. The logic of this wish which goes, you might say, with the structure of your Organization leads Us to complete it with other formulas, as follows. Let no one as a member of your union be superior to others: *not one over the other*. This is the formula of equality. We know of course that there are other factors to be considered aside from mere membership in your organization, but equality is also a part of its constitution. Not that you are all equal, but here you make yourselves equal. And it may well be that for a number of you this calls for an act of great virtue. Permit Us to tell you so, as the representative of a religion that works salvation through the humility of its divine Founder. It is impossible for someone to be a brother if he is not humble. For it is pride, as inevitable as it may seem, that provokes the tensions and struggles over prestige, over domination, over colonialism, over selfishness. It is pride that shatters brotherhood.

5. Here Our message reaches its culmination and We will speak first of all negatively. These are the words you are looking for Us to say and the words We cannot utter without feeling aware of their seriousness and solemnity: *never again one against the other,* never, never again!

Was not this the very end for which the United Nations came into existence: to be against war and for peace? Listen to the clear words of a great man who is no longer with us, John Kennedy, who proclaimed four years ago: "Mankind must put an end to war, or war will put an end to mankind." There is no need for a long talk to proclaim the main purpose of your Institution. It is enough to recall that the blood of millions, countless unheard-of sufferings, useless massacres and frightening ruins have sanctioned the agreement that unites you with an oath that ought to change the future history of the world: never again war, never again war! It is peace, peace, that has to guide the destiny of the nations of all mankind!

All thanks and honor to you who have been working for peace for twenty years and have even given distinguished victims to this holy cause! All thanks and honor to you for the conflicts that you have prevented and for those that you have settled. The results of your efforts in behalf of peace right up to the last few days may not yet have been decisive, but still they deserve to have Us step forward as spokesman for the whole world and express congratulations and gratitude to you in its name.

Gentlemen, you have accomplished and are now in the course of accomplishing a great work: you are teaching men peace. The UN is the great school where people get this education and We are here in the assembly hall of this school. Anyone who takes his place here becomes a pupil and a teacher in the art of building peace. And when you go outside of this room, the world looks to you as the architects and builders of peace.

As you know very well, peace is not built merely by means of politics and a balance of power and interests. It is built with the mind, with ideas, with the works of peace. You are working at this great endeavor, but you are only at the beginning of your labors. Will the world ever come to change the selfish and bellicose outlook that has spun out such a great part of its history up to now? It is hard to foresee the future, but easy to assert that the world has to set out resolutely on the path toward a new history, a peaceful history, on that will be truly and fully human, the one that God promised to men of goodwill. The pathways are marked out before you and the first one is disarmament.

If you want to be brothers, let the arms fall from your hands. A person cannot love with offensive weapons in his hands. Arms, and especially the terrible arms that modern science has provided you, engender bad dreams, feed evil sentiments, create nightmares, hostilities, and dark resolutions even before they cause any victims and ruins. They call for enormous expenses. They interrupt projects of solidarity and of useful labor. They warp the outlook of nations. So long as man remains the weak, changeable, and even wicked being that he so often shows himself to be, defensive arms will, alas, be necessary. But your courage and good qualities urge you on to a study of means that can guarantee the security of international life without any recourse to arms. This is an aim worthy of your efforts, and this is what peoples expect from you. This is what you have to achieve! And if it is to be done, everyone's confidence in this institution must increase and its authority must increase, and then, let us hope, its aim will be achieved. You will win the gratitude of the peoples of the world, who will be relieved of burdensome expenditures for armaments and delivered from the nightmare of ever-imminent war.

We know—and how could We help rejoicing over this—that many of you have given favorable consideration to the suggestion in behalf of peace that We issued to all nations from Bombay last December: to devote to the benefit of developing nations at least a part of the money that could be saved through a reduction of armaments. We want to repeat this suggestion now, with all the confidence inspired in Us by your sentiments of humaneness and generosity.

6. To speak of humaneness and generosity is to echo another constitutional principle of the United Nations, its positive summit: you are working here not just to eliminate conflicts between States, but to make it possible for States to work *for each other*. You are not content with facilitating coexistence between nations. You are taking a much bigger step forward, one worthy of Our praise and Our support: you are organizing fraternal collaboration between nations. You are establishing here a system of

solidarity that will ensure that lofty civilizing goals receive unanimous and orderly support from the whole family of nations, for the good of each and all. This is the finest aspect of the United Nations Organization, its very genuine human side. This is the ideal that mankind dreams of during its pilgrimage through time; this is the greatest hope of the world. We would even venture to say that it is the reflection of the plan of God—a transcendent plan full of love—for the progress of human society on earth, a reflection in which We can see the Gospel message turning from something heavenly to something earthly. Here We seem to hear an echo of the voice of Our predecessors, and especially of Pope John XXIII, whose message in *Pacem in Terris* met with such an honored and significant response among you.

What you are proclaiming here are the basic rights and duties of man, his dignity, his liberty and above all his religious liberty. We feel that you are spokesmen for what is loftiest in human wisdom—We might almost say its sacred character—for it is above all a question of human life, and human life is sacred; no one can dare attack it. It is in your Assembly, even where the matter of the great problem of birth rates is concerned, that respect for life ought to find its loftiest profession and its most reasonable defense. Your task is so to act that there will be enough bread at the table of mankind and not to support an artificial birth control that would be irrational, with the aim of reducing the number of those sharing in the banquet of life.

But it is not enough to feed the hungry. Each man must also be assured a life in keeping with his dignity, and that is what you are striving to do. Is this not the fulfillment before Our eyes, and thanks to you, of the prophet's words that apply so well to your Institution: "They shall beat their swords into plowshares and their spears into pruning-hooks" (*Is* 2, 4)? Are you not employing the prodigious forces for the earth and the magnificent inventions of science no longer as instruments of death but as instruments of life for the new era of mankind?

We know with what increasing intensity and effectiveness the United Nations Organization and the world bodies dependent upon it are working where needed to help governments speed up their economic and social progress.

We know with what ardor you are working to conquer illiteracy and to spread culture in the world, to give men modern health service adapted to their needs, to put the marvelous resources of science, technology, and organization at the service of man. All this is magnificent and deserves everyone's praise and support including Our own.

We would also like to set an example Ourself, even if the smallness of Our means might prevent anyone from appreciating the practical and quantitative significance of it. We want to see Our own charitable institutions undergo a new development in the struggle against hunger and toward meeting the main needs of the world. This is the way and the only way to build peace.

7. One word more, Gentlemen, one last word. The edifice you are building does not rest on purely material and terrestrial foundations, for in that case it would be a house built on sand. It rests most of all upon consciences. Yes, the time has come for "conversion," for personal transformation, for interior renewal. We have to get used to a new way of thinking about man, a new way of thinking about man's community life, and last of all a new way of thinking about the pathways of history and the destinies of the world. As St. Paul says, we must "put on the new man, which has been created according to God in justice and holiness of truth" (*Eph* 4, 23).

The hour has come when a pause, a moment of recollection, reflection, you might say of prayer, is absolutely needed so that we may think back over our common origin, our history, our common destiny. The appeal to the moral conscience of man has never before been as necessary as it is today, in an age marked by such great human progress. For the danger comes neither from progress nor from science; if these are used well they can, on the contrary, help to solve a great number of the serious problems besetting mankind. The real danger comes from man, who has at his disposal ever more powerful instruments that are as well fitted to bring about ruin as they are to achieve lofty conquests.

To put it in a word, the edifice of modern civilization has to be built on spiritual principles, for they are the only ones capable not only of supporting it, but of shedding light on it and inspiring it. And We are convinced, as you know, that these indispensable principles of higher wisdom cannot rest on anything but faith in God. Is he the unknown God of whom St. Paul spoke to the Athenians on the Areopagus—unknown to those who, without suspecting it, were nevertheless looking for Him and had Him close beside them, as is the case with so many men of our times? For us, in any case, and for all those who accept the ineffable revelation that Christ has made to us of Him, He is the living God, the Father of all men.

Dorothy Day
1897–1980

Dorothy Day was born in Brooklyn at the close of the last century, on November 8, 1897. She was the third of five children of a journeyman sportswriter from the South whose own father had been a Confederate army surgeon in the Civil War. Her mother's family were Northerners, from the upper Hudson Valley and from Massachusetts. The Days lived in Brooklyn and in California and in Chicago, where she was baptized in the Episcopal Church. She finished high school at age sixteen, and eventually she attended the University of Illinois at Urbana, where in 1914 as a freshman she joined the Socialist Party.

Two years later she set off for New York. She worked as a writer for the Socialist daily *The Call* and carried the union card of the Industrial Workers of the World (I.W.W.). She interviewed the radicals of her day, from Leon Trotsky to Margaret Sanger, and moved to a short-lived editorial position with *The Masses* of Max Eastman and John Reed, which ended when the government suppressed the publication for sedition. She proceeded to march with suffragists and was jailed in Washington, D.C., for participating in an anti-war demonstration.

It appears that 1917–1918 was the beginning of her conversion to apostolic zeal. She became the inseparable companion of Eugene O'Neill, but broke from his circle after one of its number committed suicide. Increasingly, she found comfort in Scripture and in mere unstructured worship, often at St. Joseph's Church in the Village. She worked during 1918 as a nurse at Kings County Hospital in Brooklyn, fell desperately in love with a man much older, and aborted the child they conceived. She traveled from place to place and from job to job; later she worked as a writer for the *Liberator,* the successor to *The Masses.* The proceeds of her autobiographical novel *The Eleventh Virgin* allowed her to purchase a small Staten Island bungalow, and she soon entered into a common-law marriage with Forster Batterham. Scripture again touched her, and she wanted more and more to pray. Batterham, a biologist, wanted none of religion. She became pregnant in 1925 with their daughter, Tamar Teresa, whom she was determined to have baptized Catholic.

That was the first light between her and Batterham. Within a year there was an ocean between them. They separated. She immediately became Catholic, having been tutored by a Sister Aloysius whom she met on the beach. She reported her pain at having left the cause of the poor to join the Church of power and of privilege. Her prayerful ambivalence seems to have ended with her meeting Peter Maurin in 1932, who held to the conviction that the trouble with the world was the separation of its theories from the Gospel. So politics, so economics, so sociology would better serve all and especially the poor if they were rooted in the Gospel.

With Peter Maurin she founded The Catholic Worker Movement, a lay apostolate imbedded in and representative of the principal of subsidiarity—decentralized, cooperative and communal decision-making and work. It has Houses of Hospitality in over sixty U.S. cities along with several communal farms in various parts of the country.

The movement itself promotes pacifism and voluntary poverty, and the hallmark of both the movement and the Houses of Hospitality is inclusiveness and respect: no one is to be made to feel like an outsider. Day and Maurin popularized the term "personalism"—serving people one by one, directly. They saw they whom they served as "ambassadors of God" who gave them the very opportunity to serve. She founded *The Catholic Worker,* a small tabloid newspaper begun in 1933 that presents the news and spreads the concept of The Catholic Worker Movement to this day.

Dorothy Day's radical Christianity was rooted in her radical devotion to the Church. She was absolutely and completely given over to the other no matter her interior state. For her, voluntary poverty was the complete turning over of self to God, the elimination of the self-interest that demands what otherwise could be used to alleviate the sufferings of others. She recognized the commonality of the sufferings of all people and especially of all women: "young and old, even in the busiest of our lives, we women especially are victims of the long loneliness. Men may go away and become desert fathers, but there were no desert mothers."[1]

Her life is writ large in her newspaper columns and books, but it is made up of countless small kindnesses all centered on recognizing the suffering Christ in those whom she met and served. Her criticisms of the systems of power, be they government, military or Church, always centered on their inability to reach the people on whom they depended for their existence and whom they were required to serve. In 1951, eighteen years after the founding of *The Catholic Worker*, Dorothy was called to the chancery offices of the Archdiocese of New York, where an aide to Francis Cardinal Spellman informed her she should have to drop "Catholic" from the name of the newspaper. She wrote back that she sincerely doubted that people would confuse the Archdiocese of New York with *The Catholic Worker*, and refused to change its name.

She wrote six books and over fifteen hundred articles, essays, and reviews. Reading what she wrote and what she did is clearly instructive of the connections between social justice and peace, so much so that the current Cardinal-Archbishop of New York has looked approvingly on efforts to canonize Dorothy Day.

From *From Union Square to Rome*[2]

A mystic may be called a man in love with God. Not one who loves God, but who is *in love with God*. And this mystical love, which is an exalted emotion, leads one to love the things of Christ. His footsteps are sacred. The steps of His passion and death are retraced down through the ages. Almost every time you step into a Church you see people making the Stations of the Cross. They meditate on the mysteries of His life, death, and resurrection, and by this they are retracing with love those early scenes and identifying themselves with the actors in those scenes.

When we suffer, we are told we suffer with Christ. We are "completing the sufferings of Christ." We suffer His loneliness and fear in the garden when His friends slept. We are bowed down with Him under the weight of not only our own sins but the sins of each other, of the whole world. We are those who are sinned against and those who are sinning. We are identified with Him, one with Him. We are members of His Mystical Body.

Often there is a mystical element in the love of a radical worker for his brother, for his fellow worker. It extends to the scene of his sufferings, and those spots where he has suffered and died are hallowed. The names of places like Everett, Ludlow, Bisbee, South Chicago, Imperial Valley, Elaine, Arkansas, and all those other places where workers have suffered and died for their cause have become sacred to the worker. You know this feeling as does every other radical in the country. Through ignorance, perhaps, you do not acknowledge Christ's name, yet, I believe you are trying to love Christ in His poor, in His persecuted ones. Whenever men have laid down their lives for their lives for their fellows, they are doing it in a measure for Him. This I still firmly believe, even though you and others may not realize it.

"Inasmuch as ye have done it unto one of the least of these brethren, you have done it unto me." Feeling this as strongly as I did, is it any wonder that I was led finally to the feet of Christ?

I do not mean at all that I went around in a state of exaltation or that any radical does. Love is a matter of the will. You know yourself how during a long strike the spirit falters, how hard it is for the leaders to keep up the morale of the men and to keep the fire of hope burning within them. They have a hard time sustaining this hope themselves. Saint Teresa says that there are three attributes of the soul: memory, understanding, and will. These very leaders by their understanding of the struggle, how victory is gained very often through defeat, how every little gain benefits the workers all over the country, through their memory of past struggles, are enabled to strengthen their wills to go on. It is only by exerting these faculties of the soul that one is enabled to love one's fellow. And this strength comes from God. There can be no brotherhood without the Fatherhood of God.

Take a factory where fifty per cent of the workers themselves content, do not care about their fellows. It is hard to inspire them with the idea of solidarity. Take those workers who despise their fellow-worker, the Negro, the Hungarian, the Italian, the Irish, where race hatreds and nationalist feelings persist. It is hard to overcome their stubborn resistance with patience and with love. That is why there is coercion, the beating of scabs and strikebreakers, the threats and the hatreds that grow up. That is why in labor struggles, unless there is a wise and patient leader, there is disunity, a rending of the Mystical Body.

"More About Holy Poverty. Which Is Voluntary Poverty."[3]

The Catholic Worker, February 1945, 1–2.

CLARIFICATION of thought is the first plank in the Catholic Worker Program.

There can be no revolution without a theory of revolution, Peter Maurin quotes Lenin as saying. Action must be preceded by thought: There is such a thing as the heresy of good works, "these accursed occupations," as St. Bernard calls them, which keep people from thinking. To feed the hungry, clothe the naked and shelter the harborless without also trying to change the social order so that people can feed, clothe and shelter themselves, is just to apply palliatives. It is to show a lack of faith in ones fellows, their responsibilities as children of God, heirs of heaven.

Of course, "the poor we will always have with us." That has been flung in our teeth again and again, usually with the comment, "so why change things which our Lord said would always be?" But surely He did not intend that there would be quite so many of them. We also have to repeat that line now that war is on and there is plentiful occupation.

"Surely, these men on your breadline, these men living in your house, could get work if they really wanted to?" And again and again we must say, "The poor ye have always with you." These are the lame, the halt, the blind, those injured in industrial accidents and those who have been driven to drink by our industrial order and the refugees and veterans from class, race and international war. There are those, too, who refuse to cooperate in this social order, who prefer to work here with us without salary. We could not do without them.

The great message which Peter Maurin has for the world today is the message of voluntary poverty, a message which he has preached by word and example. He is the most truly poor one among us. And because he has chosen to be poor, he has remained free; he has had time to think. He has lived a rich and abundant life because of that very poverty. "I think your most vital message is the praise of poverty," John Cort writes this month. But it is the most misunderstood message.

"Poverty and Pacifism" was misunderstood, and quite a few letters came in about it, but they were without rancor. On the other hand, "Cake and Circuses," which I wrote for the October issue just before the election, called forth many protests. "That you personally could have had part in it or sanctioned it, I cannot believe," one reader writes. "That *The Catholic Worker* should have been the instrumentality of its dissemination troubles me— how deep you will divine from the fact that I write you now and in so profoundly disturbed a mood, even after the passing of so many months." (This letter came in February.)

To answer this letter I shall have to reprint most of it, and then of course, my answer will not satisfy.

"That mothers of six children can 'go on a binge of department store buying, movies and cigarettes, candies and radio, and even sometimes a car,' all on one hundred and eighty dollars month, strikes me as ridiculous, certainly the six children and their mother will not live very long 'If they just do without the necessities,' and the limits of 'running up debts' are not very remote, surely. From the former heads of the A.M.A. (does he mean the American Manufacturers' Association?) such matter would not seem strange, but it is almost unthinkable coming from a group concerned with the welfare of the poor and disadvantaged. But I find equal cause for concern, the nature of *The Catholic Worker* considered, in the fact that this editorial should have been published on the very eve of the presidential election and that in it *The Catholic Worker* should have written that Mr. Roosevelt would be elected by the votes of 'millions who are bought and paid for.'

"Frankly, I cannot conceive that the bitterest partisanship could have stooped much lower. To print such an editorial under the caption of 'Comments on the news in the light of faith,' is to be guilty of sacrilege to write of it as done in the light of the 'folly of the cross' is blasphemy."

This is a comparatively mild letter compared to another received from a priest whose mother raised a large family and who is now receiving money from the three sons who are away at war.

First of all, let me apologize for the brevity of the editorial, which surely should have been clarified and treated at much greater length. It is no wonder that people misunderstand, and it is no wonder that such brevity, such shortness, sounds arrogant, and uncharitable. We owe it to our kind and charitable readers to try to explain at greater length what in our stupidity, and presumption we wrote so briefly.

In the first place, it shocks US that so many do not understand those basic principles of personalism, personal responsibility and voluntary poverty which have for the past twelve years been emphasized monthly in *The Catholic Worker* and in the lives of those who have worked in our thirty-two houses and ten farms. (Now there are ten houses and ten farms.)

I will try to explain. Samuel Johnson said that a pensioner was a slave of the state. That is his definition in his famous dictionary. Of course, he himself was glad of his pension, human nature being what it is, and poverty being hard as it is.

We believe that social security legislation, now hailed as a great victory for the poor and for the worker, is a great defeat for Christianity. It is an acceptance of the idea of force and compulsion. It is an acceptance of Cain's statement, on the part of the employer. "Am I my brother's keeper?" Since the employer can never be trusted to give a family wage, nor take care of the worker as he takes care of his machine when it is idle, the state must enter in and compel help on his part. Of course, economists say that business cannot afford to act on Christian principles. It is impractical, uneconomic. But it is generally coming to be accepted that such a degree of centralization as ours is impractical, and that there must be decentralization. In other words, business has made a mess of things, and the state has had to enter in to rescue the worker from starvation.

Of course, Pope Pius XI said that, when such a crisis came about, in unemployment, fire, flood, earthquake, etc., the state had to enter in and help.

But we in our generation have more and more come to consider the state as bountiful Uncle Sam. "Uncle Sam will take care of it all. The race question, the labor question, the unemployment question." We will all be registered and tabulated and employed or put on a dole, and shunted from clinic to birth control clinic. "What right have people who have no work to have a baby?" How many poor Catholic mothers heard that during those grim years before the war!

Of course, it is the very circumstances of our lives that lead us to write as we do. We see these ideas worked out all around us. We see the result of this way of thinking on all sides. We live with the poor, we are of the poor. We know their virtues and their vices. We know their generosities and their extravagances. Their very generosity makes them extravagant and improvident.

Please do not think we are blaming the poor when we talk so frankly about their failings, which they, too, will acknowledge. They do not want people to be sentimental about them. They do not want people to idealize them. I think they realize pretty well that they are but dust, and one of our jobs, too, is to make them realize that they are also a little less than the angels.

We are not being uncharitable to them when we talk about a binge or department store buying. Did I say that? What I meant was installment-plan buying. Who do we blame for such installment-plan buying, for the movies, cigarettes, radio, magazines, or all the trash, the worthless trash with which they try to comfort their poor hard lives. We do not blame them, God knows. We blame the advertising men, the household loan companies, the cheap stores, the radio, the movies.

The people are seduced, robbed, stupefied, drugged and demoralized daily. They are robbed just as surely as though those flat pocketbooks of those shabby mothers were pilfered of the pennies, dimes and nickels by sneak thieves.

The people say proudly, "We got It coming to us. We pay taxes. This ain't charity. It's justice." And they hug their sweets, their liquor, their movies, their radio, their dissipations to them, in a vain endeavor to find forgetfulness of the cold and ugliness, the leaking plumbing, the cold water, the lack of coal, the ugly housing, the hideous job, or if they are housewives who stay at home, from the wet diapers, the smelly clothes and beds, the shoddy mattresses and blankets and furniture that the children break to pieces, the crowded quarters where the poor mothers' heads reverberate with the din of the not too healthy children.

Yes, they pay taxes, and it is the city and the state and the federal government that is robbing them and pilfering them, too. They are taxed for every bite they eat, every shoddy rag they put on. They are taxed on their jobs, there are deductions for this and that, there are the war bonds, eighteen dollars for a twenty-five dollar war bond, paid on the installment plan. And they are not only being taxed, but they are being seduced. Their virtue is being drained from them. They are made into war profiteers, they are forced into the position of usurers. The whole nation, every man woman and child, is forced to become a profiteer-hideous word-in this war.

Some of our readers wrote indignantly, "Do you think $180 is exorbitant for the government to pay? They should be paying much more. I do not see how they can live on that, prices being what they are."

What I tried to say was that that puny, insignificant $180 which looms tremendous in the minds of the poor, was not enough for essentials. Could they rent a decent house to live in? Or could they buy a house? Pope Pius said that as many of the workers as possible should become owners. Is there any chance to become an owner on a hundred and eighty dollars a month?

Peter Maurin likes to talk about the treason of the intellectuals. With the expose of waste and inefficiency on the part of government, of graft and the spoils system ("You take this job in return for the help you gave me in getting elected") I should say that not only advertising men, not only the manufacturer robs and cheats the poor, but also the government. How quickly graft and scandals are forgotten! In Russia graft, corruption and waste in government circles are considered treason, and men have paid for it with their lives. And our Catholic employers and politicians speak at Communion breakfasts, and as long as they prosper they are held in honor; as long as they are in power they are respected. They go to Communion, they go to Mass. You must not judge them. If you speak ill of them, you are being uncharitable.

Yes, the poor have been robbed of the good material things of life, and when they asked for bread, they have been given a stone. They have been robbed of a philosophy of labor. They have been betrayed by their teachers and their political leaders. They have been robbed of their skills and made tenders of the machine. They cannot cook; they have been given the can. They cannot spin or weave or sew—they are urged to go to Klein's and get a dress for $4.98.

Bought and paid for? Yes, bought and paid for by their own most generous feelings of gratitude. Of course, they feel grateful. In spite of their talk about taxes and justice, they are grateful to the good, kind government that takes care of them. St. Teresa said that she was of so grateful a temperament she could be bought with a sardine. St. Ignatius said that love is an exchange of gifts. The government gives its paternal care and the people give their support to that particular governing body. Naturally they do not want change.

But who is to take care of them if the government does not? That is a question in a day when all are turning to the state, and when people are asking, "Am I my brother's keeper?" Certainly we all should know that it is not the province of the government to practice the works of mercy, or go in for insurance. Smaller bodies, decentralized groups, should be caring for all such needs.

The first unit of society is the family. The family should look after its own and, in addition, as the early fathers said, "every home should have a Christ room in it, so that hospitality may be practiced." "The coat that hangs in your closet belongs to the poor." "If your brother is hungry, it is your responsibility."

"When did we see Thee hungry, when did we see Thee naked?" People either plead ignorance or they say "It is none of my responsibility." But we are all members one of another, so we are obliged in conscience to help each other. The parish is the next unit, and there are local councils of the St. Vincent de Paul Society. Then there is the city, and the larger body of charitable groups. And there are the unions, where mutual aid and fraternal charity is also practiced. For those who are not Catholics there are lodges, fraternal organizations, where there is a long tradition of charity. But now there is a dependence on the state. Hospitals once Catholic are subsidized by the state. Orphanages once supported by Catholic charity receive their aid from community chests. And when it is not the state it is bingo parties!

The poor mother of six cannot reject the $180. She cannot say, "Keep your miserable, puny, insufficient $180 which you give me in exchange for my husband." She has poverty, involuntary poverty.

But we must reject it. We must keep on talking about voluntary poverty, and holy poverty, because it is only it we can consent to strip ourselves that we can put on Christ. It is only if we love poverty that we are going to have the means to help others. If we love poverty we will be free to give up a job, to speak when we feel it would be wrong to be silent. We can only talk about voluntary poverty because we believe Christians must be fools for Christ. We can only embrace voluntary poverty in the light of faith.

"The Scandal of the Works of Mercy"[4]

The spiritual works of mercy are: to admonish the sinner, to instruct the ignorant, to counsel the doubtful, to comfort the sorrowful, to bear wrongs patiently, to forgive all injuries, and to pray for the living and the dead.

The corporal works are to feed the hungry, to give drink to the thirsty, to clothe the naked, to ransom the captive, to harbor the harborless, to visit the sick, and to bury the dead.

When Peter Maurin talked about the necessity of practicing the works of mercy, he meant all of them, and he envisioned houses of hospitality in poor parishes in every city of the country, where these precepts of Our Lord could be put into effect. He pointed out that we have turned to State responsibility through home relief, social legislation and social security, and we no longer practice personal responsibility for our brother, but are repeating the words of the first murderer, "Am I my brother's keeper?" Not that our passing the buck is as crude as all that. It was a matter of social enlightenment, Holy Mother the City taking over, Holy Mother the State taking the poor to herself, gathering them to her capacious bosom studded with the jewels of the taxation of the rich and the poor alike, the subtle war between Church and State meanwhile going on at all times, in the field of education, charity, the family. In the last fifteen years the all-encroaching State, as the Bishops of the United States have called it, has gained the upper hand.

In our fight against such a concept of Christian charity, we have been accused of lining up with Wall Street and private enterprise, and the rich opponents of state control and taxation. But, anarchists that we are, we want to decentralize everything and delegate to smaller bodies and groups what can be done far more humanly and responsibly through mutual aid, as well as charity, through Blue Cross, Red Cross, union cooperation, parish cooperation.

Peter Maurin, the founder of *The Catholic Worker,* was very much an apostle to the world today, not only to the poor. He was a prophet with a social message and he wanted to reach the people with it. To get to the people, he pointed out it was necessary to embrace voluntary poverty, to strip yourself, which would give you the *means* to practice the works of mercy. To reach the man in the street you must go to the street. To reach the workers, you begin to study a philosophy of labor, and take up manual labor, useful labor, instead of white collar work. To be the least, to be the worker, to be poor, to take the lowest place and thus be the spark which would set afire the love of men towards each other and to God (and we can only show our love for Good by our love for our fellows). These were Peter's ideas, and they are indispensable for the performing of the works of mercy.

When Father Lombardi spoke of few weeks ago in St. Patrick's Cathedral and on the Fordham campus, he spoke of the need to make a new social order. He was making no anti-communist speech, he said. He was making no nationalist speech. He was speaking a gospel of love, and that meant here and now a redistribution of this world's goods so that a man could have as many children as God sent him, and support them, have a home for them and work for them to do. This world's goods do not belong to any one nation, any few men, he pointed out.

We are all devoured by a passion for social justice today, and seeking an alternative to Communism and capitalism. We like to discuss capitalism, industrialism, distributism, decentralization—all the work that is being done by the National Catholic Welfare Conference in Washington and by the National Catholic Rural Life Conference, but with this tremendous work of indoctrination, with all this work which goes on in conference, convention, classroom, and through periodicals, much of it comes to words and not very vital words at that.

Peter liked to talk of making a message dynamic, and that meant with him putting it into practice. There was simple common sense in his argument that if you want to reach the man in the street, you go out on a park bench with him, you go out to well your paper on the street just as the Jehovah's Witnesses do, just as the communists do.

Publishing a paper and reaching the man in the street, was to Peter, performing the first four of the spiritual works of mercy. To go on picket lines, was to perform spiritual works of mercy. It was to dramatize by a supplicatory procession the needs of the worker, the injustice perpetrated against him. To bear wrongs patiently, yes, but not to let the bosses continue in the sin of exploiting you. To forgive the injury, yes, but to try to do away with the injury.

I remember one time when we were all picketing in the National Biscuit Company strike on West Fourteenth Street. There was a mass picket line which extended around the block, and the police began to break it up, and then the scabs arrived in taxi cabs and the mob started to boo, and the whole affair began to look ugly. As we gave out our literature, Frank O'Donnell, who is now one of the members of the farming community at St. Benedict's Farm at Upton, Mass., turned to us all and said mildly, winking at Peter, "Don't forget we are all gentle personalities!"

It reminded me of the Communist who shouted at me as we were dispersed by the police at another demonstration, and there was a brutal show of force by the police: "What about a little brotherly love, sister?"

Yes, such works of mercy, such spiritual works of mercy, can be dangerous, and can smack of class war attitudes. And of that we are often accused, because the performance of the works of mercy finds us on the side of the poor, the exploited, whether with literature, picketing, soup kitchen, etc. As Evelyn Waugh said to us plaintively last spring, "Don't you think the rich suffer too?" And there is indeed plenty of room for the works of mercy there. Perhaps we are also carrying out that apostolate too. Perhaps some of the rich are reading *The Catholic Worker*. After all, THE COMMONWEAL must have readers who are able to afford the things advertised in its columns, such as jewels, laces and fur coats, which puts them definitely out of the class of the Fourteenth Street reader and shopper whom we cater to.

We are always accused of going to extremes and perhaps it does seem like an extreme to be talking of the street apostolate and the retreat apostolate in the same breath. Yet they go together. In the attempt to perform these works of mercy, which are far more difficult than the immediate physical ones of feeding and clothing and sheltering, we came to the decision after ten years of work in city and country throughout the land that we needed a retreat house for the work. We had had colloquiums for the clarification of thought, and tired of wrangling, we had tried an annual retreat for all the leaders of The Catholic Worker Houses in the United States; so many came, and the response was so great, that we decided to have a year-round retreat house where we could raise what we needed as much as possible, where we could build up our very good library, where we could have a house of studies for those who wanted to stay longer than the week's retreat on the farm.

The first project was at Easton, and never was there such a retreat house. Generous priests gave us their time, and came and slept in unheated rooms and dormitories. At first there was no running water, but one valiant priest, Father Pacifique Roy, S.S.J., who had been a missionary both in Quebec and Louisiana and accustomed to working with his hands, directed the work by example as well as by precept, and we dug ditches and laid pipe and soon had running water on every floor of the barn and the house. We had electricity in every room, and the electrical work was done by Father Roy and our men. During the war, when it was all but impossible to get men or materials, we had the genius of this priest who knew how to use all odds and ends of pipe and wire and make up gadgets to take the place of those we could not get. If Father Roy could have been spared to us (he is invalided in Canada right now) we would have had a lumber mill, a cement block plant and a grist mill and electricity from our own windmill, and all such contrivances of human ingenuity for our farm retreat house.

As it is, we have become more bourgeois and comfortable, but not more self-sufficient. We have a long way to go to exemplify the poverty of a St. Francis or a Peter Maurin.

People out of jails and out of hospitals, men from the bread-line and from the road, readers of the paper from all walks of life, students, priests too, come to make retreats with us. We have a chapel in which the stations of the cross, the statues of the Blessed Mother and St. Joseph are made by our own artists. Adé de Bethune carved the crucifix over the altar, and the altar and benches were made by one of the men who came in from the Bowery, an old carpenter with a bitter tongue, who so despised the unskilled poor that whenever anyone gave any evidence of any skill, he would say sourly, "And what jail did you learn that in?"

This old man nearing eighty had his little shop and house right at the entrance to our farm at Easton where we first had retreats, and unlike the porter at the gate described by St. Benedict, old Maurice had quite a different tongue. I used to feel sad that instead of seeing Christ in each guest who came, he saw the bum, and so greeted us, one and all. He was a good example of "The Friend of the Family," "The Man Who Came to Dinner." And also a fitting member of our community, which is country-wide by now, and which Stanley Vishnewsky has come to call "*the contemptibles.*" "It is a new order I started," he is going around saying. But it is really Peter Maurin who started it. Stanley just named it.

Our retreat house now is at Newburgh, New York, sixty-five miles up the Hudson River and although we are not permanent there, I wish to write about it in some detail, because I have written two other articles for THE COMMONWEAL on the Houses of Hospitality where works of mercy are performed.

We are intending to sell the place at Newburgh and buy one on some bay near New York where we can fish and so cut down our expenses. Fishing and clamming and beachcombing are occupations more agreeable to man then farming. We want a twenty acre place so that we can have a large garden and orchard. We do not need the ninety-six acres we have now at Newburgh. We had offered the opportunity to three couples to build there on our acreage, but the offer was not taken up because of the cost of building materials and the lack of skills among the men. Also, because most of those who are contemplating the land movement are still thinking in terms of farms that "pay," whereas we are thinking of a village and town economy and a combination of land and crafts, and the use of the machine only insofar as it is the extension of the hand of man and so under his control, making things of use to others; in other words, a political economy based on the consumers' needs rather than the producers' profits.

It will be seen that our concept of the works of mercy, including as it does making the kind of society where the "rich man becomes poor, and the poor holy," a society where there is no unemployment, and where each can "work according to his ability and receive according to his need," is a foretaste of heaven indeed.

We have had retreats every other week these past two years at Maryfarm, Newburgh, and in the winter when we are limited to the house alone and have to give up the barns and the carriage house and the tents, then the house becomes a rest house as well as a house of studies, and there are always those out of hospitals who need rest and care, sickness of mind and body that need to be nursed.

We have daily Mass at the Farm, and we are permitted by the Chancery Office to have the Blessed Sacrament at all times while a priest is with us and we are blessed in having an invalided priest visiting us these past fifteen months or so. We have Prime and Compline, we have sung Masses for all the big feast days, we have reading at the table during retreats, and sometimes when there is no retreat but a feast day to be celebrated. There are many visitors, and it is very much a crowded inn and hospice during all the months of the year. Jane O'Donnell is in charge of the House, and John Fillinger of the Farm, and Hans Tunnesen takes care of cooking and carpentry alternately. Both the latter are seamen and have been with us for years. I remember the gibe (a friendly one) of one of our friends once who was combatting our idea of farming communes where the family could enjoy a combination of private and communal property. "Instead of a family commune," he said, "they are running a home for celibate seamen." This was at the time of the first seamen's strike and many were staying with us.

There are families among us who do not have much time for many of the works of mercy any longer outside their own families, though they are always contributors of food and clothing to our community of contemptibles. And it is indeed true that there are many celibates, willing and unwilling ones, among us.

Converts come to work with us who might have preferred family life but are barred from it by a previous bad marriage. There will always be, in a way, the willing and the reluctant celibates, and for these, the community life of *The Catholic Worker*, with its men and women working together, dedicated to the common effort, affords the comfort of a home, of contacts with friends, the normal, happy relationships of men and women working together. (The men become more gentle and the women try harder to please, and in spite of the war of sexes which goes on and always will, there is a growth of the good love of friendship so sadly needed in the world today.)

The works of mercy are a wonderful stimulus to our growth in faith as well as in love. Our faith is taxed to the utmost and so grows through this strain put upon it. It is pruned again and again, and springs up bearing much fruit. For anyone starting to live literally the words of the Fathers of the Church, "the bread you retain belongs to the hungry, the dress you lock up is the property of the naked," "what is superfluous for one's need is to be regarded as plunder if one retains it for one's self," there is always a trial ahead. "Our faith, more precious than gold, must be tried as though by fire." Here is a letter we received today. "I took a gentleman seemingly in need of spiritual and temporal guidance into my home on a Sunday afternoon. Let him have a nap on my bed, went through the want ads with him, made coffee and sandwiches for him, and when he left, I found my wallet had gone also."

I can only say that the Saints would only bow their heads and not try to understand or judge. They received no thanks—well then, God had to repay them. They forebore to judge, and it was as though they took off their cloak besides their coat to give away. This is expecting heroic charity of course. But these things happen for our discouragement, for our testing. We are sowing the seed of love, and we are not living in the harvest time so that we can expect a crop. We must love to the point of folly, and we are indeed fools, as our Lord Himself was who died for such a one as this. We lay down our lives too when we have performed so painfully thankless an act, because this correspondent of ours is poor in this world's goods. It is agony to go through such bitter experiences, because we all want to love, we desire with a great longing to love our fellows, and our hearts are often crushed at such rejections. But a Carmelite nun said to me last week, "It is the crushed heart which is the soft heart, the tender heart," and maybe it is one way to become meek and humble of heart like Jesus.

Such an experience is crueller than that of our young men in Baltimore who were arrested for running a disorderly house, i.e., our St. Anthony's House of Hospitality, and who spent a few nights in jail. Such an experience is dramatic to say the least. Such an experience is crueller than that which happened to one of our men here in New York who was attacked (for his pacifism) by a maniac with a knife in our kitchen. Actually to shed one's blood is a less bitter experience.

Well, our friend has suffered from his experience and it is part of the bitterness of the poor, who cheat each other, who exploit each other, even as they are exploited. Who despise each other even as they are the despised.

And is it to be expected that virtue and destitution should go together? No, as John Cogley has written, they are the destitute in every way, destitute of this world's goods, destitute of honor, or gratitude, of love, and they need so much, that we cannot take the works of mercy apart, and say I will do this one, or that one work of mercy. We find they all go together.

Some years ago there was an article in THE COMMONWEAL by Georges Bernanos. He ended his article as I shall end mine, paraphrasing his words, and it is a warning note for these apocalyptic times:

"Every particle of Christ's divine charity is today more precious for your security—for your security, I say—than all the atom bombs in all the stock piles." It is by the works of mercy that we shall be judged.

Jessica Powers
1905–1988

Jessica Powers was a contemplative nun and poet. One might demur at the thought of a contemplative being called an apostle, but the focus of apostolic zeal need not always be directly in corporal works. Faith, especially faith lived simply, is zeal's strength. Jessica Powers truly stands with the others in this collection as one called and sent to love others deeply and individually, and to pray and act for their own developing love of God.

She was born on February 7, 1905, in Mauston, Wisconsin and died on August 18, 1988 not far away, at the Carmel of the Mother of God in Pewaukee, Wisconsin, the construction of which she supervised while prioress of the Milwaukee Carmel. Her life of silence and poetry eventuated in the publication of nearly four hundred poems. Additionally, hundreds of letters survive in private collections and in university archives.

Her four grandparents were emigrants: her mother's side Scotch and her father's side Irish. She was born the third of four children of John and Delia Trainer Powers; she had one sister and two brothers. Her older sister Dorothy died in 1916, and her father died two years later, in the spring before she began high school in Mauston. After graduation she enrolled in the Marquette University school of journalism, but left after one year and worked for a few years as a secretary in Chicago while feeding her love of poetry with reading in libraries.

When her mother died in 1925 she returned to the family farm, keeping house until her brothers John and Daniel married. Her poetry began to appear in local papers, and she contributed a column entitled "The Percolator" to *The Milwaukee Sentinel*. She left the farm in 1936, first going to Chicago and then, in 1937, to New York, where she lived with Jessie and Anton Pegis and entered into the Catholic literary circle that surrounded them. In New York she published her first book, *The Lantern Burns*, which includes some of her best work, including "The Master Beggar," a deep evocation of the call of an apostle.

Always a poet, she began her formal contemplative life in 1941 at age thirty-six. She entered the Milwaukee Carmel, became Sister Miriam of the Holy Spirit, and was perpetually professed in 1946. That year she published her second book of poems, *The Place of Splendor* (1946). Four additional books of poetry, *The Little Alphabet* (1955), *Mountain Sparrow* (1972), *Journey to Bethlehem* (1980), and her collected works in *The House at Rest* (1984) preceded the *Selected Poetry of Jessica Powers* (1989).

She was elected prioress three times, in 1955, in 1958, and in 1964. Tuberculosis claimed her for one year, and she had to leave the Carmel for a sanitarium from October 1959 through October 1960, returning to her duties as prioress shortly after the new year, 1961. Her poems and her letters show her closeness to the rhythms of the earth. She wrote one fall: "But there is something spiritual about autumn, a lovely sadness, an estrangement from earth, a loneliness of soul; it has a mood that brings one closer to God."[1] In the dead of winter, she wrote the temperature was 25 degrees below zero and, "It is good to live out here so close to the weather; people that live close to the weather and depend upon it should surely find it easier to depend on God."[2] Wisconsin weather apparently affected her deeply, and she appears to have traveled to better climes occasionally. Her life was truly cloistered, but she spent some time in later years at the Carmels of Reno, Sante Fe, and San Diego, and attended a few conferences on contemplative religious life.

It is evident from her poetry, and more so from her letters, that she was well aware of the contemporary lights in the Church. She mentions in her letters reading the work of Daniel Berrigan, Teilhard de Chardin, Thomas Merton, Bernard Cooke, Dr. Tom Dooley, contemporary psychologists, and theorists of religious life, along with the writings of Teresa of Avila, John of the Cross, and Jean-Pierre de Caussade. She read what contemporary poetry she could, including Federico Garcia Lorca, but her rule restricted her from reading anything that was strictly news or current events. Church news reached her, and she showed delight at Vatican II: "This should be a new year of wonderful happenings, don't you think? I am sure the Holy Spirit will not let the valuable work of the Council be destroyed or diminished."[3]

She lived her own advice. The seasons completed themselves annually in her writing: "July always seems the season of grace in a unique way. God is present in His sounding waters and wooded valleys if we but had the leisure to 'taste and see.'"[4] She maintained a lively and deeply spiritual correspondence with many persons, including Sr. Margaret Ellen Traxler, S.S.N.D., founder of the Institute of Women Today in Chicago, from whose papers the letter selections are taken.

From *Letters*

St. John the Baptist, 1959

Our poor souls—how they are torn to pieces in this hurried and disordered world—and how they would like to "bed down in God" and be all at peace.

August 18, probably 1964

I was delighted to see the commentary on the Gospels and to be able to read Lorca's poetry, but I did not think the book on automation would quite fit into our lives. I decided to sample it though and was quite overwhelmed. Chapter 12 is simply terrific—one of those things that could fill the mind for days or a lifetime. I thought of Our Holy Mother St. Teresa who was so moved by word of what Lutheranism was doing that the reform of Carmel practically was born of that—what would she say now of a Godless world? It is the saddest of tragedies. . . .

Lorca's poetry, as I sip it, fits into this immense sadness. Where will the world go, without God? And what can we do to help?

August 22, 1973

I am studying St. John of the Cross again and love the ideal of union with God to which he urges us. The escape from self-love. It is like new inspiration. Don't you think life has a number of calls—here and there a new "Go forth" like Abraham's. And we tear up our roots and go.

December 16, 1976

Life happens, someone said, while you are making other plans. How often we go where we did not expect to go.

From *The House at Rest*

"The Place of Splendor"

Little one, wait.
Let me assure you this is not the way
to gain the terminal of outer day.

Its single gate
lies in your soul, and you must rise and go
by inward passage from what earth you know.

The steps lead down
through valley after valley, far and far
past the five countries where the pleasures are,

And past all known
maps of the mind and every colored chart
and past the final outcry of the heart.

No soul can view
its own geography; love does not live
in places open and informative,

Yet, being true,
it grants to each its Raphael across
the mist and night through unknown lands of loss.

Walk till you hear
light told in music that was never heard,
and softness spoken that was not a word.

The soul grows clear
when senses fuse: sight, touch and sound are one
with savor and scent, and all to splendor run.

The smothered roar
of the eternities; their vast unrest
and infinite peace are deep in your own breast.

That light-swept shore
will shame the data of grief upon your scroll.
Child, have none told you? *God* is in your soul.

From *Selected Poetry of Jessica Powers*

"The Master Beggar"

Worse than the poorest mendicant alive,
the pencil man, the blind man with his breath
of music shaming all who do not give,
are You to me, Jesus of Nazareth.

Must You take up Your post on every block
of every street? Do I have no release?
Is there no room of earth that I can lock
to Your sad face, Your pitiful whisper "Please"?

I seek the counters of time's gleaming store
but make no purchases, for You are there.
How can I waste one coin while you implore
with tear-soiled cheeks and dark blood-matted hair?

And when I offer You in charity
pennies minted by love, still, still You stand
fixing Your sorrowful wide eyes on me.
Must all my purse be emptied in Your hand?

Jesus, my beggar, what would You have of me?
Father and mother? the lover I longed to know?
The child I would have cherished tenderly?
Even the blood that through my heart's valves flow?

I too would be a beggar. Long tormented,
I dream to grant You all and stand apart
with You on some bleak corner, tear-frequented,
and trouble mankind for its human heart.

From *The House at Rest*

"Letter of Departure"

"There is nothing in the valley, or home, or street
                              worth turning back for—
nothing!" you write. O bitter words and true
to seed the heart and grow to this green answer:
let it be nothing to us that we knew
streets where the leaves gave sparsely of the sun
or white small rested houses and the air
strung with the sounds of living everywhere.
The mystery of God lies before and beyond us,
so bright the sight is dark, and if we halt
to look back once upon the burning city,
we shall be paralyzed by rage or pity,
either of which can turn the blood to salt.

We knew too much of the knowable dark world,
its secret and its sin,
too little of God. And now we rise to see
that even our pledges to humanity
were false, since love must out of Love begin.
Here where we walk the fire-strafed road and thirst
for the great face of love, the blinding vision,
our wills grow steadfast in the heart's decision
to keep the first commandment always first.
We vow that nothing now shall give us cause
to stop and flounder in our tears again,
that nothing—fire or dark or persecution
or the last human knowledge of all pain—
shall turn us from our goal.

With but the bare necessities of soul—
no cloak or purse or scrip—let us go forth
and up the rocky passes of the earth,
crying, "Lord, Lord", and certain presently

(when in the last recesses of the will
and in the meshes of the intellect
the quivering last sounds of earth are still)
to hear an answer that becomes a call.
Love, the divine, Love, the antiphonal,
speaks only to love,
for only love could learn that liturgy,
since only love is erudite to master
the molten language of eternity.

From *Selected Poetry of Jessica Powers*

"Abraham"

I love Abraham, that old weather-beaten
unwavering nomad; when God called to him,
no tender hand wedged time into his stay.
His faith erupted him into a way
far-off and strange. How many miles are there
from Ur to Haran? Where does Canaan lie,
or slow mysterious Egypt sit and wait?
How could he think his ancient thigh would bear
nations, or how consent that Isaac die,
with never an outcry nor an anguished prayer?
I think, alas, how I manipulate
dates and decisions, pull apart the dark,
dally with doubts here and with counsel there,
take out old maps and stare.
Was there a call at all, my fears remark.
I cry out: Abraham, old nomad you,
are you my father? Come to me in pity.
Mine is a far and lonely journey, too.

From *The House at Rest*

"Counsel for Silence"

Go without ceremony of departure
and shade no subtlest word with your farewell.
Let the air speak the mystery of your absence

and the discerning have their minor feast
on savory possible or probable.
Seeing the body present, they will wonder
where went the secret soul, by then secure
out past your grief beside some torrent's pure
refreshment. Do not wait to copy down
the name, much less address, of who might need you.
Here you are pilgrim with no ties of earth.
Walk out alone and make the never-told
your healing distance and your anchorhold.
And let the ravens feed you.

Franz Jägerstätter
1907–1943

Franz Jägerstätter was born in St. Radegund, Austria, in 1907 and was beheaded by the Third Reich after a military trial on August 9, 1943.[1] His thirty-six years neither began nor ended in fame; he was by all accounts a simple Austrian peasant. He had a reputation for being a bit on the wild side as a young man, but in 1936 he married a young woman who lived nearby. They honeymooned in Rome, and after his marriage he seemed to have undergone a spiritual awakening.

While he was politically nonpartisan, he was openly anti-Hitler. Two years after his marriage Hitler invaded Austria and Jägerstätter stood alone in his village voting against the *Anschluss*. He quite clearly declared his intent not to fight with Hitler's army. Despite his having undergone at least one and probably two periods of military training as required, he refused additional military training, was imprisoned in Linz, then in Berlin, and beheaded.

His story was relatively unknown outside German-speaking nations until an American sociologist, Gordon Zahn, happened to meet a former prison chaplain who had written a book about Franz Reinisch, a Catholic priest executed for refusing allegiance to Adolf Hitler. An appendix to that book spoke of "Franz II," and Zahn pursued the story of Franz Jägerstätter, whom he considered a martyr-saint.

Jägerstätter was the church sexton in the Catholic village of St. Radegund, which lay mostly unknown not thirty kilometers from Linz-an-der-Donau, the birthplace of both Adolf Hitler and Adolf Eichmann. Fifty-seven men of the tiny village lost their lives in World War II. Only one hundred families lived there; it was probably impossible for anyone not to know about Franz Jägerstätter.

He had left his schooling at age fourteen, although his excellence in religion and reading both followed him and charted his course. He was a faithful husband and father; by the time he left St. Radegund for the last time he had three daughters, the eldest about six years old.

The increasing depth of his belief was evident in his work and in his writing. He left a remarkable testament of his faith in the form of a letter to his godson, a letter to his pastor on leaving St. Radegund, seventeen letters to his wife from prison, nine essays or commentaries, a statement of his position, and a final farewell letter immediately prior to his execution. In one of his farewell messages, he wrote "I can say from my own experience how painful life often is when one lives as a halfway Christian; it is more like vegetating than living."[2]

Franz Jägerstätter was one of six Catholics executed for their conscientious objection to service under Hitler. His sacrifice remains misunderstood by many, and unknown to many more. By 1992 the Church began to formally recognize that fact when the Austrian bishops voted unanimously to ask for his beatification. Austrian towns and cities have named streets for him; there are plays, poems, films. His witness, as recorded by Gordon Zahn, caused Daniel Ellsberg to release the Pentagon Papers, thereby changing the United States political-military course concerning Vietnam.[3]

What follows are selections from his Prison Statement and from his Commentaries, as translated by Gordon Zahn.

From *In Solitary Witness*

The Crooked Game

Are not almost all of us playing a more or less crooked game these days? Do we not know that all of us must prove ourselves to be good and precious fruit if we wish to enter the Kingdom of Heaven? In this regard it is impossible for dishonesty to lead to perfection.

When and how is one dishonest? First, when one presents himself to his fellow men as being something other than what he really is; second, when one constantly acts in a manner different from what he really thinks, says, or writes. But is it at all possible today to speak or act as one thinks? Granted, there are times when one acts differently from the way he thinks for reasons of obedience, but this obedience should never go so far as to oblige one to perform acts that are actually evil. We know God does not demand the impossible of us, even considering the times in which we live today. We need not always act, then, exactly as we think. We need not always speak our mind; one can and may keep silent—up to a certain point. For it would certainly lead to trouble if one always told his neighbor just what he thought of him, so it is sometimes better to hold one's tongue and maintain silence. One need not always speak out—indeed, many find it unpleasant to listen when someone talks too much while they themselves have to keep silent for the time being.

True, it is doubly hard not to be dishonest when one lives in a country where freedom of belief is restricted. If dishonesty were not harmful to our efforts to attain eternal blessedness, what difference would it make whether or not one has freedom of belief? Or is dishonesty wrong even if we injure no one by it? Most certainly yes—if only because we generally, in fact always, injure ourselves. For though we cannot hurt God by our falseness (we can only offend Him), we can hurt His Church.

An old saying goes: "As one lives, so shall he die." And thus it can often happen that many are not able to give up this crooked game even at the moment of death. How harshly will they be judged who no longer go to church or receive Holy Communion—or finally leave the Church and even persecute other Christians? It is certain that they will never possess the Kingdom of Heaven unless they reform their ways. But such people who have shown so clearly where they stand have at least partially abandoned their crooked game; and I would wager that they will not have to suffer anywhere near as great an agony in hell as those who have swindled their whole lives through, always trying to deceive their spiritual leaders and their closest associates. Did not Christ Himself say, "Had you been hot or cold, I would have kept you near Me; but because you are only lukewarm, I will spit you out of My mouth"?

There will also be some who think, why should I be honest with men who are without doubt bad characters and not honest with me either? The first answer is that we should never repay evil with evil. Secondly, we have no more right to be dishonest with such a person, just because he is probably no good, than we would with someone who is good; for, in the eyes of God, the bad man is just as much my brother as the man who is good. Or if we have a mission to help such a person better himself so that we may deserve to be considered good Christians and, by so doing, prove ourselves to be even slightly better than those we look down upon—then we must also show ourselves to be honest and upright with others, even when we are rewarded for our pains with ridicule and scorn.

So, we should not be surprised if one can often hear it said, "That's the way they are." By playing our crooked game, we actually bring serious scandal down upon the whole Catholic Church, since all of us are usually spoken of as a single entity. And how do we rate at this moment in this matter of integrity? Is a man upright and sincere when, on the one hand, he is a member of the NVP or some other Nazi organization and makes sacrifices for it and takes up collections for it while, at the same time, he wishes the whole outfit would fade away and disappear? I think many have the idea that they can fool the others in this way, but we ought not to think our opponents are so stupid. They know full well that someone who still fulfills his Sunday obligations and gives some semblance of being religious in other ways has to be cheating somebody, since no one can serve two masters at the same time. For a while, of course, they will let it ride, since they know that such people really fool nobody but themselves and, in the process, do the greatest damage to themselves and to the Church. Needless to say, they will rarely trust such double-dealers with important political appointments.

Does there remain even the possibility for us to convert others when we so generally co-operate with everything the Party wishes or commands of us—just so we can hold on to some temporal advantage? What must people of other faiths think of us and our faith if it means so little to us?

Actually, we should be ashamed of ourselves in comparison with the truly committed Party member who, for his part, even though his faith was rooted only in worldly things, fought for his ideals and for his National Socialist ideology in the face of all prohibitions and did not even fear prison or death. Would they have achieved their victory if they had been as timid and cowardly as we Catholics of Germany are today?

But we Catholics apparently entertain hopes of winning a glorious victory for our faith without any battle—and, to top it all, we expect to do this after first fighting for the enemy and helping him win his victory! Can anyone really believe such a thing is possible? In my opinion such a thing has never happened throughout the whole history of the world. Modern man, of course, is very inventive, but if he has progressed so far as to discover a way of winning a victory without a struggle, I have not yet heard of it.

The Prison Statement

These few words are being set down here as they come from my mind and my heart. And if I must write them with my hands in chains, I find that much better than if my will were in chains. Neither prison nor chains nor sentence of death can rob a man of the Faith and his free will. God gives so much strength that it is possible to bear any suffering, a strength far stronger than all the might of the world. The power of God cannot be overcome. If people took as much trouble to warn men against the serious sins which bring eternal death, and thus keep them from such sins, as they are taking to warn me against a dishonorable death, I think Satan could count on no more than a meager harvest in the last days. Again and again, people stress the obligations of conscience as they concern my wife and children. But I can not believe that, just because one has a wife and children, he is free to offend God by lying (not to mention all the other things he would be called upon to do). Did not Christ Himself say: "He who loves father, mother, or children more than Me is not deserving of My love"? Or, "Fear not those who can kill the body but not the soul; rather fear much more those who seek to destroy body and soul in hell."

For what purpose, then, did God endow all men with reason and free will if, despite this, we have to render blind obedience; or if, as so many also say, the individual is not qualified to judge whether this war started by Germany is just or unjust? What purpose is served by the ability to distinguish between good and evil? I would be ready to show blind obedience, but only in such a case where one would not injure others in the process. If God had not given me the grace and strength even to die for my faith if I have to, I, too, would probably be doing the same as most other Catholics. There are probably many Catholics who think they would be suffering and dying for the faith only if they had to suffer punishment for refusing to renounce the Catholic Church. But I believe that everyone who is ready to suffer and die rather than offend God by even the slightest venial sin also suffers for his faith. And by so doing, I believe such a one can earn even a far greater reward in heaven than does one faced with the command to renounce the Catholic Church—for, in the latter situation, one is obliged under pain of mortal sin to choose death in preference to apostasy even when the apostasy would be one of mere external appearance. A saint once said, "If one were able to extinguish the fires of hell by telling only one 'white lie' he should not tell it; for that 'white lie' would itself be an offense against God." Such an idea seems utterly ridiculous in the 19th [*sic*] century if one judges by the thoughts and speech of so many. It is true, we humans have certainly changed a great deal in our faith as compared with the early Christians; but God has not on this account removed even one iota from his Commandments—even though we will soon be able to date our writings in the year 2000.

I can easily see that anyone who refuses to acknowledge the Nazi Folk Community and also is unwilling to comply with all the demands of its leaders will thereby forfeit the rights and privileges offered by that nation. But it is not much different with God: he who does not wish to acknowledge the community of saints or who does not obey all the commandments set forth by Him and His Church and who is not ready to undergo sacrifices and to fight for His Kingdom either—such a one also loses every claim and every right under that Kingdom. Of course, God often grants a long reprieve before He exacts the death penalty. As soon as a man commits a mortal sin, he is condemned to eternal death, at least until he confesses that sin or, if he has no opportunity to do this, erases it by an act of perfect contrition. But if a sinner does not amend his life and reform, then finally one fine day the death sentence will be executed without any advance warning. But there remains this great difference: not only does such a sinner die the earthly death to which we are all condemned but, more than this, he is condemned to eternity in hell as well.

Now anyone who is able to fight for both kingdoms and stay in good standing in both communities (that is, the community of saints and the Nazi Folk Community) and who is able to obey every command of the Third Reich—such a man, in my opinion, would have to be a great magician. I for one cannot do so. And I definitely prefer to relinquish my rights under the Third Reich and thus make sure of deserving the rights granted under the Kingdom of God. It is certainly unfortunate that one cannot spare his family this sorrow. But the sorrows of this world are short-lived and soon pass away. And this sorrow is not at all comparable to those that Jesus was not able to spare His dear Mother in His sufferings and death.

Is, then, the Kingdom of God of such slight value that it is not worth some sacrifice, that we place every little thing of this world ahead of the eternal treasures? Did not the Apostle Paul say, "No eye has seen and no ear has heard and the heart of man has no hint of what God has prepared for those who love Him"? And once when St. Augustine wanted to write a book about the joys of heaven, St. Jerome (who, it was later learned, had died that very day) appeared and said to him: "Just as certainly as you cannot grasp the entire world in one hand, so can you never contain the joys of heaven in one book." So unimaginably great are these joys that God has prepared for us in His Kingdom— and the greatest of all is that these joys will last forever. I believe we would almost go out of our minds with joy if someone were to tell us that we could be sure that in a few days all these joys of heaven would be ours on earth and would last for a billion years. Yet what are a billion years in comparison with eternity? Not as much as a half second compared with an entire day. If the whole world consisted of nothing but grains of sand, and once every thousand years one bird would come and each time carry away a single grain of sand, one could scarcely imagine how many years would have to pass before the whole world would disappear in this slow process—still one day it would disappear; but in comparison with eternity this would still be nothing. It is absolutely impossible for man to think of any example which would even come close to a comparison with eternity.

But not only the joys of heaven are eternal; this holds, too, for the terrible tortures of hell. As the Saviour once said, "Cast them out into the exterior darkness; there will be wailing and the gnashing of teeth." In the same way, the pains of hell will be so great that one simply cannot compare them at all with earthly sufferings—and, moreover, they, too, will last for all eternity.

Should it be too much for us, then, to submit ourselves completely, in our short lifetime on earth, to the commandments of God and His Church (which, besides, can serve to bring men temporal blessings and prosperity as well, if one brings God sacrifices and self-denial)? Ask the nonbeliever if he has no sorrows on this earth or if he has everything his heart desires or can do what and how he pleases. Would it have been at all possible, even once in our lifetime, to offend God by a serious sin if we had considered and believed more firmly in eternity and the bitter sufferings of Jesus Christ? If Christ had not come into this world and had not died for us, heaven would have remained closed to us, no matter how virtuous and chaste we might have been in our lives. Even though Jesus saw our meanness and ingratitude already before His passion and knew, too, that for many His bitter sufferings and death would be wasted, still He took this heavy sorrow upon Himself. The love God has for us men is so great that we can never hope to comprehend it with our human reason. And, yet, it is possible for us in our hearts— often for considerations of the slightest earthly advantages and prestige—to offend so good a dear Lord and God who suffered so for us and who promises such an unimaginably great reward if only we keep His commandments and love Him!

What, then, can an earthly master offer us in this world? And, yet, there are immediate and severe penalties for anyone who does not follow his regulations or who seriously offends such a high personage. Is it too much, then, if the Lord of heaven and earth, Who has borne so much for us and in addition promised so great a reward, should banish us to hell if we offend Him seriously—especially when He is always ready to forgive if we but ask for forgiveness and make a good resolution to reform? Consider what great efforts and sacrifices so many of us men are prepared to make to gain worldly esteem, or an athlete to win a prize. If we were to make the same efforts to gain heaven, there would be many and great saints. For the Kingdom of Heaven, too, will not be ours without effort and sacrifice. Christ has said Himself that the Kingdom of Heaven can be won only by those who storm it and take it by force. Or, again, "Enter by the narrow gate, for wide is the gate and broad the road that leads to ruin and many are those who go therein. How small is the gate and how narrow the way which leads to life, and how few are they who find it."

Why do we give so little thought to eternity? Why is it so hard for us to make sacrifices for Heaven? Yes, even though we cannot see it, we are sometimes clearly aware of the presence of an invisible power which makes every conceivable effort to lead man along the path to ruin. And that is the power of hell. Lucifer knows full well what joys and glories there are in heaven, but since he himself can never return to them, he cannot bear man to know such joy. For this reason, he and his companions use every means to bind all our thoughts and desires to this world. The less we think of eternity and of God's love and mercy, the more likely Satan is to win his game. For us men there are only two possibilities in this world: either we become ever better or ever worse; there is simply no such thing as standing still. Yes, even for those who have worked hard to come ever closer to God, there can be many reverses, just as an army advancing toward its victory does not win all its battles but must endure many defeats. Nevertheless, this does not mean that the struggle should be given up as hopeless; instead, one must pick himself up with renewed strength and strive on again toward the desired goals.

Therefore, just as the man who thinks only of this world does everything possible to make life here easier and better, so must we, too, who believe in the eternal Kingdom, risk everything in order to receive a great reward there. Just as those who believe in National Socialism tell themselves that their struggle is for survival, so must we, too, convince ourselves that our struggle is for the eternal Kingdom. But with this difference: we need no rifles or pistols for our battle, but, instead, spiritual weapons—and the foremost among these is prayer. For prayer, as St. Clare says, is the shield which the flaming arrows of the Evil One cannot pierce. Through prayer we constantly implore new grace from God, since without God's help and grace it would be impossible for us to preserve the Faith and be true to His commandments.

The true Christian is to be recognized more in his works and deeds than in his speech. The surest mark of all is found in deeds showing love of neighbor. To do unto one's neighbor what one would desire for himself is more than merely not doing to others what one would not want done to himself. Let us love our enemies, bless those who curse us, pray for those who persecute us. For love will conquer and will endure for all eternity. And happy are they who live and die in God's love.

Teresa of Calcutta
1910–1997

Agnes Gonxha Bojaxhiu, the third child of an Albanian grocer and his wife, was born in Skopje, Macedonia, in 1910. Her plain beginnings followed her throughout her life. As her first biographer, Malcolm Muggeridge wrote, "God has turned these qualities to his own ends. I never met anyone less sentimental, less scatty, more down-to-earth."[1]

At seventeen Agnes followed her long held desire to be a missionary and entered the Irish Sisters of Loreto in Dublin, traveled to Darjeeling for further training, and then settled in Calcutta, where for seventeen years she taught and served as principal of her order's St. Mary's High School. Part of her teaching included current events. The teaming Calcutta slums outside the convent walls were full of street urchins and lepers, and she could not willingly ignore their suffering. She had professed her final vows as a Sister of Loreto in 1937, but nine years later, while on a long train ride to a combined retreat and recuperative period from possible tuberculosis, she recognized a call within her call to religious life: "It was a second calling. It was a vocation to give up even Loreto where I was very happy and to go out in the streets to serve the poorest of the poor."[2]

Two years later she received permission to leave the Sisters of Loreto to pursue her vocation to help the poor under the jurisdiction of the Archbishop of Calcutta. Her first step was to train with the Medical Missionary Sisters in Patna, India. She then gathered the children of the slums into her open-air schools. With donors and volunteers, many of them her former students, she built the foundation for what became the Missionaries of Charity. Begun with twelve women in 1950 as a diocesan congregation, and recognized as a pontifical order fifteen years later, the Missionaries of Charity now number 1,800 in 150 houses in 25 countries around the world.

The poor of Calcutta radicalized her devotion to the life of God within all whom she met. She described the first woman she rescued from an anonymous street death: "She had been half eaten up by the rats and ants. I took her to the hospital, but they could not do anything for her. They only took her because I refused to move until they accepted her. From there I went to the municipality and I asked them to give me a place where I could bring these people, because on the same day I had found other people dying in the streets."[3] In 1952 she received permission from Calcutta officials to use the abandoned temple to Kali, the Hindu goddess of transition and destroyer of demons, to house her Kalighat Home for the Dying, which she named Nirmal Hriday ("Pure Heart"). There she began to gather the dying destitute from Calcutta streets so that they might die with dignity. Since then approximately forty-two thousand people have been taken to Nirmal Hriday, where nineteen thousand of them have died.

Mother Teresa, as she came to be called, is both an annoyance and a challenge to the world of middle-class comfort. She pledged free service to the poor; she and her sisters vowed poverty, chastity, obedience, and a fourth vow to give "whole hearted free service to the poorest of the poor— to Christ in his distressing disguise."[4] She refused any payment for the services of her order; all the resources of the community are donated.

Her simplicity and directness remain as disarming now as when she was alive. Her philosophy is rooted in the absolute sacredness of human life—at the United Nations' Third Special Session on Disarmament she responded to the media's questions on nuclear weapons by saying the abortion was a far more serious threat to world peace. There and elsewhere her recommendations centered on showing love for others: "The biggest disease today is not leprosy or tuberculosis, but rather the feeling of being unwanted, uncared for and deserted by everybody. The greatest evil is the lack of love and charity, the terrible indifference towards one's neighbor who lives at the roadside assaulted by exploitation, corruption, poverty and disease."[5]

Her mission was to spread Christian love, not to enhance government service. She was implacable whenever anyone questioned the need for greater resources of personnel and money to meet the ever-expanding dilemma of the poor of Calcutta's slums. But it was not for her to direct government programs; she often said that welfare was for a purpose, but love was for a person.

At the time of her death in 1997, Mother Teresa was among the most recognized women in the world. She merited multiple awards in life: the Pope John XXIII Peace Prize (1971), the Nobel Prize (1979), and the U.S. Presidential Medal of Freedom (1985) among them. Her Nobel Prize speech is reprinted below.

Most of her published works are collections of her sayings. Inevitably, whenever and wherever she spoke, she found a way to make the point that abortion was the deepest sin scraping humanity's soul. For her, the respect for life in all forms, especially those most defenseless *in utero*, was basic to both world and personal peace.

From *In My Own Words*

God does not demand that I be successful. God demands that I be faithful.

When facing God, results are not important. Faithfulness is what is important.[6]

Today it is very fashionable to talk about the poor. Unfortunately, it is not fashionable to talk with them.[7]

God has created us to do small things with great love. I believe in that great love, that comes, or should come from our heart, should start at home: with my family, my neighbors across the street, those right next door. And this love should then reach everyone.[8]

Nobel Prize Acceptance Speech, 1979

As we have gathered here together to thank God for the Nobel Peace Prize, I think it will be beautiful that we pray the prayer of St Francis of Assisi which always surprises me very much. We pray this prayer every day after Holy Communion, because it is very fitting for each one of us. And I always wonder that 400–500 years ago when St Francis of Assisi composed this prayer, they had the same difficulties that we have today as we compose this prayer that fits very nicely for us also. I think some of you already have got it—so we will pray together:

Let us thank God for the opportunity that we all have together today, for this gift of peace that reminds us that we have been created to live that peace, and that Jesus became man to bring that good news to the poor. He, being God, became man in all things like us except in sin, and he proclaimed very clearly that he had come to give the good news.

The news was peace to all of good will and this is something that we all want—the peace of heart. And God loved the world so much that he gave his son—it was a giving; it is as much as if to say it hurt God to give, because he loved the world so much that he gave his son. He gave him to the Virgin Mary, and what did she do with him?

As soon as he came in her life, immediately she went in haste to give that good news, and as she came into the house of her cousin, the child—the unborn child—the child in the womb of Elizabeth, lept with joy. He was, that little unborn child was, the first messenger of peace. He recognised the Prince of Peace, he recognised that Christ had come to bring the good news for you and for me. And as if that was not enough—it was not enough to become a man—he died on the cross to show that greater love, and he died for you and for me and for that leper and for that man dying of hunger and that naked person lying in the street not only of Calcutta, but of Africa, and New York, and London, and Oslo—and insisted that we love one another as he loves each one of us. And we read that in the Gospel very clearly: "love as I have loved you; as I love you; as the Father has loved me, I love you." And the harder the Father loved him, he gave him to us, and how much we love one another, we too must give to each other until it hurts.

It is not enough for us to say: "I love God, but I do not love my neighbor." St John says that you are a liar if you say you love God and you don't love your neighbor. How can you love God whom you do not see, if you do not love your neighbor whom you see, whom you touch, with whom you live? And so this is very important for us to realize that love, to be true, has to hurt.

It hurt Jesus to love us. It hurt him. And to make sure we remember his great love, he made himself the bread of life to satisfy our hunger for his love—our hunger for God—because we have been created for that love. We have been created in his image. We have been created to love and be loved, and he has become man to make it possible for us to love as he loved us. He makes himself the hungry one, the naked one, the homeless one, the sick one, the one in prison, the lonely one, the unwanted one, and he says: "You did it to me." He is hungry for our love, and this is the hunger of our poor people. This is the hunger that you and I must find. It may be in our own home.

I never forget an opportunity I had in visiting a home where they had all these old parents of sons and daughters who had just put them in an institution and forgotten, maybe. And I went there, and I saw in that home they had everything, beautiful things, but everybody was looking toward the door. And I did not see a single one with a smile on their face. And I turned to the sister and I asked: How is that? How is it that these people who have everything here, why are they all looking toward the door? Why are they not smiling?

I am so used to see the smiles on our people, even the dying ones smile. And she said: "This is nearly every day. They are expecting, they are hoping that a son or daughter will come to visit them. They are hurt because they are forgotten." And see—this is where love comes. That poverty comes right there in our own home, even neglect to love. Maybe in our own family we have somebody who is feeling lonely, who is feeling sick, who is feeling worried, and these are difficult days for everybody. Are we there? Are we there to receive them? Is the mother there to receive the child?

I was surprised in the West to see so many young boys and girls given into drugs. And I tried to find out why. Why is it like that? And the answer was: "Because there is no one in the family to receive them." Father and mother are so busy they have no time. Young parents are in some institution and the child goes back to the street and gets involved in something. We are talking of peace. These are things that break peace.

But I feel the greatest destroyer of peace today is abortion, because it is a direct war, a direct killing, direct murder by the mother herself. And we read in the scripture, for God says very clearly: "Even if a mother could forget her child, I will not forget you. I have curved you in the palm of my hand." We are curved in the palm of his hand; so close to him, that unborn child has been curved in the hand of God. And that is what strikes me most, the beginning of that sentence, that even if a mother *could* forget, something impossible—but even if she could forget—I will not forget you.

And today the greatest means, the greatest destroyer of peace is abortion. And we who are standing here—our parents wanted us. We would not be here if our parents would do that to us.

Our children, we want them, we love them. But what of the other millions. Many people are very, very concerned with the children of India, with the children of Africa where quite a number die, maybe of malnutrition, of hunger and so on, but millions are dying deliberately by the will of the mother. And this is what is the greatest destroyer of peace today. Because if a mother can kill her own child, what is left for me to kill you and you to kill me? There is nothing between.

And this I appeal in India, I appeal everywhere—"Let us bring the child back"—and this year being the child's year: What have we done for the child? At the beginning of the year I told, I spoke everywhere and I said: Let us ensure this year that we make every single child born, and unborn, wanted. And today is the end of the year. Have we really made the children wanted?

I will tell you something terrifying. We are fighting abortion by adoption. We have saved thousands of lives. We have sent word to all the clinics, to the hospitals, police stations: "Please don't destroy the child; we will take the child." So every hour of the day and night there is always somebody—we have quite a number of unwedded mothers—tell them: "Come, we will take care of you, we will take the child from you, and we will get a home for the child." And we have a tremendous demand for families who have no children, that is the blessing of God for us. And also, we are doing another thing which is very beautiful.

We are teaching our beggars, our leprosy patients, our slum dwellers, our people of the street, natural family planning.

And in Calcutta alone in six years—it is all in Calcutta—we have had 61,273 babies less from the families who would have had them because they practice this natural way of abstaining, of self-control, out of love for each other. We teach them the temperature method which is very beautiful, very simple. And our poor people understand. And you know what they have told me? "Our family is healthy, our family is united, and we can have a baby whenever we want." So clear—those people in the street, those beggars—and I think that if our people can do like that how much more you and all the others who can know the ways and means without destroying the life that God has created in us.

The poor people are very great people. They can teach us so many beautiful things. The other day one of them came to thank us and said: "You people who have evolved chastity, you are the best people to teach us family planning because it is nothing more than self-control out of love for each other." And I think they said a beautiful sentence. And these are people who maybe have nothing to eat, maybe they have not a home where to live, but they are great people.

The poor are very wonderful people. One evening we went out and we picked up four people from the street. And one of them was in a most terrible condition. And I told the Sisters: "You take care of the other three; I will take care of this one that looks worse." So I did for her all that my love can do. I put her in bed, and there was such a beautiful smile on her face. She took hold of my hand, as she said one word only: "thank you"— and she died.

I could not help but examine my conscience before her. And I asked: "What would I say if I was in her place?" And my answer was very simple. I would have tried to draw a little attention to myself. I would have said: "I am hungry, I am dying, I am cold, I am in pain," or something. But she gave me much more—she gave me her grateful love. And she died with a smile on her face—like that man who we picked up from the drain, half eaten with worms, and we brought him to the home—"I have lived like an animal in the street, but I am going to die like an angel, loved and cared for." And it was so wonderful to see the greatness of that man who could speak like that, who could die like that without blaming anybody, without cursing anybody, without comparing anything. Like an angel—this is the greatness of our people.

And that is why we believe what Jesus has said: "I was hungry, I was naked, I was homeless; I was unwanted, unloved, uncared for—and you did it to me."

I believe that we are not really social workers. We may be doing social work in the eyes of the people. But we are really contemplatives in the heart of the world. For we are touching the body of Christ twenty-four hours. We have twenty-four hours in his presence, and so you and I. You too must try to bring that presence of God into your family, for the family that prays together stays together. And I think that we in our family, we don't need bombs and guns, to destroy or to bring peace—just get together, love one another, bring that peace, that joy, that strength of presence of each other in the home. And we will be able to overcome all the evil that is in the world. There is so much suffering, so much hatred, so much misery, and we with our prayer, with our sacrifice are beginning at home. Love begins at home, and it is not how much we do, but how much love we put in the action that we do. It is to God almighty—how much we do does not matter, because he is infinite, but how much love we put in that action. How much we do to him in the person that we are serving.

Some time ago in Calcutta we had great difficulty in getting sugar. And I don't know how the word got around to the children, and a little boy of four years old, a Hindu boy, went home and told his parents: "I will not eat sugar for three days. I will give my sugar to Mother Teresa for her children." After three days his father and mother brought him to our house. I had never met them before, and this little one could scarcely pronounce my name. But he knew exactly what he had come to do. He knew that he wanted to share his love.

And this is why I have received such a lot of love from all. From the time that I have come here I have simply been surrounded with love, and with real, real understanding love. It could feel as if everyone in India, everyone in Africa is somebody very special to you. And I felt quite at home, I was telling Sister today. I feel in the convent with the Sisters as if I am in

Calcutta with my own Sisters. So completely at home here, right here.

And so here I am talking with you. I want you to find the poor here, right in your own home first. And begin love there. Be that good news to your own people. And find out about your next-door neighbor. Do you know who they are?

I had the most extraordinary experience with a Hindu family who had eight children. A gentleman came to our house and said: "Mother Teresa, there is a family with eight children; they have not eaten for so long; do something." So I took some rice and I went there immediately. And I saw the children—their eyes shining with hunger. I don't know if you have ever seen hunger. But I have seen it very often. And she took the rice, she divided the rice, and she went out. When she came back I asked her: "Where did you go, what did you do?" And she gave me a very simple answer: "They are hungry also." What struck me most was that she knew—and who are they? a Muslim family— and she knew. I didn't bring more rice that evening because I wanted them to enjoy the joy of sharing.

But there were those children, radiating joy, sharing the joy with their mother because she had the love to give. And you see this is where love begins—at home. And I want you—and I am very grateful for what I have received. It has been a tremendous experience and I go back to India—will be back by next week, the 15th I hope, and I will be able to bring your love.

And I know well that you have not given from your abundance, but you have given until it has hurt you. Today the little children, they gave—I was so surprised—there is so much joy for the children that are hungry. That the children like themselves will need love and get so much from their parents.

So let us thank God that we have had this opportunity to come to know each other, and that this knowledge of each other has brought us very close. And we will be able to help the children of the whole world, because as you know our Sisters are all over the world. And with this prize that I have received as a prize of peace, I am going to try to make the home for many people that have no home. Because I believe that love begins at home, and if we can create a home for the poor, I think that more and more love will spread. And we will be able through this understanding love to bring peace, be the good news to the poor. The poor in our own family first, in our country and in the world.

To be able to do this, our Sisters, our lives have to be woven with prayer. They have to be woven with Christ to be able to understand, to be able to share. Today, there is so much suffering and I feel that the passion of Christ is being relived all over again. Are we there to share that passion, to share that suffering of people—around the world, not only in the poor countries. But I found the poverty of the West so much more difficult to remove.

When I pick up a person from the street, hungry, I give him a plate of rice, a piece of bread, I have satisfied. I have removed that hunger. But a person that is shut out, that feels unwanted, unloved, terrified, the person that has been thrown out from society—that poverty is so hurtful and so much, and I find that very difficult. Our Sisters are working amongst that kind of people in the West.

So you must pray for us that we may be able to be that good news. We cannot do that without you. You have to do that here in your country. You must come to know the poor. Maybe our people here have material things, everything, but I think that if we all look into our own homes, how difficult we find it sometimes to smile at each other, and that the smile is the beginning of love.

And so let us always meet each other with a smile, for the smile is the beginning of love, and once we begin to love each other, naturally we want to do something. So you pray for our Sisters and for me and for our Brothers, and for our co-workers that are around the world. Pray that we may remain faithful to the gift of God, to love him and serve him in the poor together with you. What we have done we would not have been able to do if you did not share with your prayers, with your gifts, this continual giving. But I don't want you to give me from you abundance. I want that you give me until it hurts.

The other day I received $15 from a man who has been on his back for twenty years and the only part that he can move is his right hand. And the only companion that he enjoys is smoking. And he said to me: "I do not smoke for one week, and I send you this money." It must have been a terrible sacrifice for him but see how beautiful, how he shared. And with that money I brought bread and I gave to those who are hungry with a joy on both sides. He was giving and the poor were receiving.

This is something that you and I can do—it is a gift of God to us to be able to share our love with others. And let it be able to share our love with others. And let it be as it was for Jesus. Let us love one another as he loved us. Let us love him with undivided love. And the joy of loving him and each other—let us give now that Christmas is coming so close.

Let us keep that joy of loving Jesus in our hearts, and share that joy with all that we come in touch with. That radiating joy is real, for we have no reason not to be happy because we have Christ with us. Christ in our hearts, Christ in the poor that we meet, Christ in the smile that we give and the smile that we receive. Let us make that one point—that no child will be unwanted, and also that we meet each other always with a smile, especially when it is difficult to smile.

I never forget some time ago about fourteen professors came from the United States from different universities. And they came to Calcutta to our house. Then we were talking about the fact that they had been to the home for the dying. (We have a home for the dying in Calcutta, where we have picked up more than 36,000 people only from the streets of Calcutta, and out of that big number more than 18,000 have died a beautiful death. They have just gone home to God.) And they came to our house and we talked of love, of compassion. And then one of them asked me: "Say, Mother, please tell us something that we will remember". And I said to them: "Smile at each other, make time for each other in your family. Smile at each other."

And then another one asked me: "Are you married?" And I said: "Yes, and I find it sometimes very difficult to smile at Jesus because he can be very demanding sometimes." This is really something true. And there is where love comes—when it is demanding, and yet we can give it to him with joy.

Just as I have said today, I have said that if I don't go to heaven for anything else I will be going to heaven for all the publicity because it has purified me and sacrificed me and made me really ready to go to heaven.

I think that this is something, that we must live life beautifully, we have Jesus with us and he loves us. If we could only remember that God loves us, and we have an opportunity to love others as he loves us, not in big things, but in small things with great love, then Norway becomes a nest of love. And how beautiful it will be that from here a centre for peace from war has been given. That from here the joy of life of the unborn child comes out. If you become a burning light of peace in the world, then really the Nobel Peace Prize is a gift of the Norwegian people. God bless you!

Thomas Merton
1915–1968

Thomas Merton was a Trappist monk of the Abbey of Gethsemani, Kentucky from 1941 to 1968, when he was accidentally electrocuted near Bangkok, Thailand, where he was attending a congress of Roman Catholic monks. He was fifty-two years old.

Merton was born in Prades, France "On the last day of January 1915, under the sign of the Water Bearer, in a year of a great war, and down in the shadow of some French mountains on the borders of Spain. . . ."[1] So begins the autobiography he wrote under monastic obedience, *The Seven Storey Mountain,* which sold six hundred thousand copies its first year and remains among the best selling Christian books ever.

Merton's American mother and his New Zealander father were artists. His mother died when he was six years old, leaving him and his three-year-old brother Jean Paul to be cared for by his father and other family members. His education progressed from elementary school in Bermuda to high school in France and in England, where his father died when Merton was sixteen. He studied at Cambridge, and earned a master's degree in literature at Columbia University, where he converted to Catholicism. He taught for a short while at St. Bonaventure's University in upper New York State, where his inclinations to priesthood and religious life led him to apply to the Franciscans. They at first accepted and then rejected his interest, probably because he divulged too much about his Cambridge days and involvements. He worked for a while with the Baroness de Hueck in Harlem. In 1941 he visited the Cistercian Abbey of Gethsemani, where he entered a short time later and eventually became Father M. Louis, a Trappist monk.

There are many sides to Thomas Merton. His writings are so extensive that he is increasingly difficult to categorize. He was a poet, a learned novice master, a brilliant essayist, and a tireless correspondent. In recent years, he has become known even more intimately through the posthumous publication of his journals and his letters.

For most of his religious life he lived in his monastic community, often in deep turmoil about obedience, ever seeking what it meant for him to be a contemplative: "Sometimes I am mortally afraid. There are the days when there seems to be nothing left of my vocation—my contemplative vocation—but a few ashes. And everybody calmly tells me: 'Writing is your vocation.'"[2] And so he wrote: scores of poems, magazine articles, essays, pamphlets, translations, journals, letters, and not a few books. Throughout he was a faithful, if uncomfortable, member of his monastic community. One biographer has written that while hospitalized in Louisville he began a deep relationship with a young nurse; a letter survives in which he assures his abbot that the relationship has ended and she is engaged to be married in Chicago.[3]

For a while he was forbidden to write, and so volunteered to be master of novices. The solitude he craved came slowly: a few hours in a small building set up on the property for ecumenical dialogue, or little while in his novitiate office. After serving as master of novices, and just a few years before he died, he received permission to live full-time in the small building, now his hermitage. On January 31, 1965, he wrote: "I can imagine no greater cause for gratitude on my fiftieth birthday than that, on it, I woke up in a hermitage."[4] It was from that hermitage he continued to write on matters of race and religion, of war and of peace, as well as on monastic life. His popularity straddled the middle years of the century, and waned in some intellectual quarters as the Second Vatican Council opened in part because of his intense and expert grounding in the ancient and medieval Church Fathers.

His final journey took him to visit the poet Lawrence Ferlinghetti in San Francisco, the Dali Lama in Dhramsala, in the Himalayas, to Singapore and to Bangkok, from whence he planned to travel to Indonesia and Hong Kong. A part of the purpose of the trip was to look for places Gethsemani might establish hermitages. He died, alone, during a midday break in his cottage at the Thai Red Cross Conference Center in Samat Prakarn, apparently electrocuted by a standing electric fan.

From *The Seven Storey Mountain*[5]

So any man may be called at least *de jure,* if not *de facto,* to become fused into one spirit with Christ in the furnace of contemplation and then go forth and cast upon the earth that same fire which Christ wills to see enkindled.

This means, in practice, that there is only one vocation. Whether you teach or live in the cloister or nurse the sick, whether you are in religion or out of it, married or single, no matter who you are or what you are, you are called to the summit of perfection: you are called to a deep interior life perhaps even to mystical prayer, and to pass the fruits of your contemplation on to others. And if you cannot do so by word, then by example.

From *Contemplation in a World of Action*[6]

This is not intended merely as another apologia for an official, institutional life of prayer. Nor is it supposed to score points in an outdated polemic. My purpose is rather to examine some basic questions of *meaning.* What does the contemplative life or the life of prayer, solitude, silence, meditation, mean to man in the atomic age? What can it mean? Has it lost all meaning whatever?

When I speak of the contemplative life I do not mean the institutional cloistered life, the organized life of prayer. This has special problems of its own. Many Catholics are now saying openly that the cloistered contemplative *institution* is indefensible, that it is an anachronism that has no point in this modern world. I am not arguing about this—I only remark in passing that I do not agree. Prescinding from any idea of an institution or even of a religious organization, I am talking about a special dimension of inner discipline and experience, a certain integrity and fullness of personal development, which are not compatible with a purely external, alienated, busy-busy existence. This does not mean that they are incompatible with action, with creative work, with dedicated love. On the contrary, these all go together. A certain depth of disciplined experience is a necessary ground for fruitful action. Without a more profound human understanding derived from exploration of the inner ground of human existence, love will tend to be superficial and deceptive. Traditionally, the ideas of prayer, meditation and contemplation have been associated with this deepening of one's personal life and this expansion of the capacity to understand and serve others.

Let us start from one admitted fact: if prayer, meditation and contemplation were once taken for granted as central realities in human life everywhere, they are so no longer. They are regarded, even by believers, as somehow marginal and secondary: what counts is getting things done. Prayer seems to be nothing but "saying words," and meditation is a mysterious process which is not understood: if it has some usefulness, that usefulness is felt to be completely remote from the life of ordinary men. As for contemplation: even in the so-called "contemplative life" it is viewed with suspicion! If "contemplatives" themselves are afraid of it, what will the ordinary lay person think? And, as a matter of fact, the word "contemplation" has unfortunate resonances— the philosophic elitism of Plato and Plotinus.

It is a curious fact that in the traditional polemic between action and contemplation, modern apologists for the "contemplative" life have tended to defend it on pragmatic grounds—in terms of action and efficacy. In other words, monks and nuns in cloisters are not "useless," because they are engaged in a very efficacious kind of spiritual activity. They are not idle, lazy, evasive: they are "getting things done," but in a mysterious and esoteric sort of way, an invisible, spiritual way, by means of their prayers. Instead of acting upon things and persons in the world, they act directly upon God by prayer. This is in fact a "superior kind of activity," a "supreme efficacy," but people do not see it. It has to be believed.

I am not interested, for the moment, in trying to prove anything by this argument. I am concerned only with its meaning to modern people. Obviously there are many who *believe* this in the sense that they accept it "on faith" without quite seeing how it is possible. They accept it on authority without understanding it themselves, and without trying to understand it. The argument is not one which appeals to them. It arouses a curious malaise, but they do not know what to do about it. They put it away on a mental shelf with other things they have no time to examine.

This view of the contemplative life, which is quite legitimate as far as it goes, places a great deal of stress on the prayer of petition, on intercession, on vicarious sacrifice and suffering as work, as action, as "something accomplished" in cloisters. And stress is laid on the idea that the prayers and sacrifices of contemplatives produce certain definite effects, albeit in a hidden manner. They "produce grace" and they also in some way "cause" divine interventions. Thus it happens that a considerable volume of letters arrives in the monastery or convent mailbag requesting prayers on the eve of a serious operation, on the occasion of a lawsuit, in personal and family problems, in sickness, in all kinds of trouble. Certainly, Catholics believe that God hears and answers prayers of petition. But it is a distortion of the contemplative life to treat it as if the contemplative concentrated all his efforts on getting graces and favors from God for others and for himself.

This conception of God and of prayer is one which fits quite naturally into a particular image of the universe, a cause-and-effect mechanism with a transcendent God "outside" and "above" it, acting upon it as Absolute First Cause, Supreme Prime Mover. He is the Uncaused Cause, guiding, planning, willing every effect down to the tiniest detail. He is regarded as a Supreme Engineer. But men can enter into communication with Him, share in His plans, participate in His causation by faith and prayer. He delegates to men a secret and limited share in His activity in so far as they are united with Him.

I am not saying that there is anything "wrong" with this. I have expressed it crudely, but it is perfectly logical and fits in naturally with certain premises. However, the trouble is that it supposes an image of the universe which does not correspond with that of post-Newtonian physics. Now, in the nineteenth century and in the modernist crisis of the early twentieth century there was one response to that: "If our view of the universe does not correspond with that of modern science, then to hell with science. We are right and that's that." But since that time it has been realized that while God is transcendent He is also immanent, and that faith does not require a special ability to imagine God "out there" or to picture Him spatially removed from His Creation as a machine which He directs by remote control. This spatial imagery has been recognized as confusing and irrelevant to people with a radically different notion of the space-time continuum. Teilhard de Chardin is one witness among many—doubtless the best known—to a whole new conception, a dynamic, immanentist conception of God and the world. God is at work in and through man, perfecting an ongoing Creation. This too is to some extent a matter of creating an acceptable image, a picture which we can grasp, which is not totally alien to our present understanding, and it will doubtless be replaced by other images in later ages. The underlying truth is not altered by the fact that it is expressed in different ways, from different viewpoints, as long as these viewpoints do not distort and falsify it.

Now it happens that the immanentist approach, which sees God as directly and intimately present in the very ground of our being (while being at the same time infinitely transcendent), is actually much closer to the contemplative tradition. The real point of the contemplative life has always been a deepening of faith and of the personal dimensions of liberty and apprehension to the point where our direct union with God is realized and "experienced." We awaken not only to the realization of the immensity and majesty of God "out there" as King and Ruler of the universe (which He is) but also a more intimate and more wonderful perception of Him as directly and personally present in our own being. Yet this is not a pantheistic merger or confusion of our being with His. On the contrary, there is a distinct conflict in the realization that though in some sense He is more truly ourselves than we are, yet we are not identical with Him, and though He loves us better than we can love ourselves we are opposed to Him, and in opposing Him we oppose our own deepest selves. If we are involved only in our surface existence, in externals, and in the trivial concerns of our ego, we are untrue to Him and to ourselves. To reach a true awareness of Him as well as ourselves, we have to renounce our selfish and limited self and enter into a whole new kind of existence, discovering an inner center of motivation and love which makes us see ourselves and everything else in all entirely new light. Call it faith, call it (at a more advanced stage) contemplative illumination, call it the sense of God or even mystical union: all these are different aspects and levels of the same kind of realization: the awakening to a new awareness of ourselves in Christ, created in Him, redeemed by Him, to be transformed and glorified in and with Him. In Blake's words, the "doors of perception" are opened and all life takes on a completely new meaning: the real sense of our own existence, which is normally veiled and distorted by the routine distractions of an alienated life, is now revealed in a central intuition. What was lost and dispersed in the relative meaninglessness and triviality of purposeless behavior (living like a machine, pushed around by impulsions and suggestions from others) is brought together in fully integrated conscious significance. This peculiar, brilliant focus is, according to Christian tradition, the work of Love and of the Holy Spirit. This "loving knowledge" which sees everything transfigured "in God," coming from God and working for God's creative and redemptive love and tending to fulfillment in the glory of God, is a contemplative knowledge, a fruit of living and realizing faith, a gift of the Spirit.

The popularity of psychedelic drugs today certainly shows, if nothing else, that there is an appetite for this kind of knowledge and inner integration. The only trouble with drugs is that they superficially and transiently mimic the integration of love without producing it. (I will not discuss here the question whether they may accidentally help such integration, because I am not competent to do so.)

Though this inner "vision" is a gift and is not directly produced by technique, still a certain discipline is necessary to prepare us for it. Meditation is one of the more important characteristic forms of this discipline. Prayer is another. Prayer in the context of this inner awareness of God's direct presence becomes not so much a matter of cause and effect, as a celebration of love. In the light of this celebration, what matters most is love itself, thankfulness, assent to the unbounded and overflowing goodness of love which comes from God and reveals Him in His world.

This inner awareness, this experience of love as an immediate and dynamic presence, tends to alter our perspective. We see the prayer of petition a little differently. Celebration and praise, loving attention to the presence of God, become more important than "asking for" things and "getting" things. This is because we realize that in Him and with Him all good is present to us and to mankind: if we seek first the Kingdom of Heaven, all the rest comes along with it. Hence we worry a great deal less about the details of our daily needs, and we trust God to take care of our problems even if we do not ask Him insistently at every minute to do so. The same applies to the problems of the world. But on the other hand, this inner awareness and openness makes us especially sensitive to urgent needs of the time, and grace can sometimes move us to pray for certain special needs. The contemplative life does not ignore the prayer of petition, but does not overemphasize it either. The contemplative prays for particular intentions when he is strongly and spontaneously inspired to do so, but does not make it his formal purpose to keep asking for this and that all day long.

Now, prayer also has to be seen in the light of another fundamental experience, that of God's "absence." For if God is immanently present He is also transcendent, which means that He is completely beyond the grasp of our understanding. The two ("absence" and "presence") merge in the loving knowledge that "knows by unknowing" (a traditional term of mysticism). It is more and more usual for modern people to be afflicted with a sense of absence, desolation, and incapacity to even "want" to pray or to think of God. To dismiss this superficially as an experience of "the death of God"—as if henceforth God were completely irrelevant—is to overlook one significant fact: that this sense of absence is not a one-sided thing: it is dialectical, and it includes its opposite, namely presence. And while it may be afflicted with doubt it contains a deep need to believe.

The point I want to make is this: experience of the contemplative life in the modern world shows that the most crucial focus for contemplative and meditative discipline, and for the life of prayer, for many modern men, is precisely this so-called sense of absence, desolation, and even apparent "inability to believe." I stress the word "apparent," because though this experience may to some be extremely painful and confusing, and to raise all kinds of crucial "religious problems," it can very well be a sign of authentic Christian growth and a point of decisive development in faith, if they are able to cope with it. The way to cope with it is not to regress to an earlier and less mature stage of belief, to stubbornly reaffirm and to "enforce" feelings, aspirations and images that were appropriate to one's childhood and first communion. One must, on a new level of meditation and prayer, live through this crisis of belief and grow to a more complete personal and Christian integration by experience.

This experience of struggle, of self-emptying, "self-naughting," of letting go and of subsequent recovery in peace and grace on a new level is one of the ways in which the *Pascha Christi* (the death and resurrection of Christ) takes hold on our lives and transforms them. This is the psychological aspect of the work of grace which also takes place beyond experience and beyond psychology in the work of the Sacraments and in our objective sharing of the Church's life.

I am of course not talking about "mystical experience" or anything new and strange, but simply the fullness of personal awareness that comes with a total self-renunciation, followed by self-commitment on the highest level, beyond mere intellectual assent and external obedience.

Real Christian living is stunted and frustrated if it remains content with the bare externals of worship, with "saying prayers" and "going to church," with fulfilling one's external duties and merely being respectable. The real purpose of prayer (in the fully personal sense as well as in the Christian assembly) is the deepening of personal realization in love, the awareness of God (even if sometimes this awareness may amount to a negative factor, a seeming "absence"). The real purpose of meditation—or at least that which recommends itself as most relevant for modern man—is the exploration and discovery of new dimensions in freedom, illumination and love, in deepening our awareness of our life in Christ.

What is the relation of this to action? Simply this. He who attempts to act and do things for others or for the world without deepening his own self-understanding, freedom, integrity and capacity to love, will not have anything to give others. He will

communicate to them nothing but the contagion of his own ob-
sessions, his aggressiveness, his ego-centered ambitions, his de-
lusions about ends and means, his doctrinaire prejudices and
ideas. There is nothing more tragic in the modern world than
the misuse of power and action to which men are driven by
their own Faustian misunderstandings and misapprehensions.
We have more power at our disposal today than we have ever
had, and yet we are more alienated and estranged from the
inner ground of meaning and of love than we have ever been.
The result of this is evident. We are living through the greatest
crisis in the history of man; and this crisis is centered precisely
in the country that has made a fetish out of action and has lost
(or perhaps never had) the sense of contemplation. Far from
being irrelevant, prayer, meditation and contemplation are of
the utmost importance in America today. Unfortunately, it must
be admitted that the official contemplative life as it is lived in
our monasteries needs a great deal of rethinking, because it is
still too closely identified with patterns of thought that were accepted five hundred years ago, but which are completely strange
to modern man.

But prayer and meditation have an important part to play in
opening up new ways and new horizons. If our prayer is the expression of a deep and grace-inspired desire for newness of
life—and not the mere blind attachment to what has always
been familiar and "safe"—God will act in us and through us to
renew the Church by preparing, in prayer, what we cannot yet
imagine or understand. In this way our prayer and faith today
will be oriented toward the future which we ourselves may
never see fully realized on earth.

From *Seeds of Contemplation*[7]

In great saints you find that perfect humility and perfect integrity coincide. The two turn out to be practically the same
thing. The saint is unlike everybody else precisely because he is
humble.

As far as the accidentals of this life are concerned, humility
can be quite content with whatever satisfies the general run of
men. But that does not mean that the essence of humility consists in being just like everybody else. On the contrary, humility

consists in being precisely the person you actually are before God, and since no two people are alike, if you have the humility to be yourself you will not be like anyone else in the whole universe. But this individuality will not necessarily assert itself on the surface of everyday life. It will not be a matter of mere appearances, or opinions, or tastes, or ways of doing things. It is something deep in the soul.

To the truly humble man the ordinary ways and customs and habits of men are not a matter for conflict. The saints do not get excited about the things that people licitly eat and drink, wear on their bodies, or hang on the walls of their houses. To make conformity or non-conformity with others in these accidents a matter of life and death is to fill your interior life with confusion and noise. Ignoring all this as indifferent, the humble man takes whatever there is in the world that helps him to find God and leaves the rest aside.

He is able to see quite clearly that what is useful to him may be useless for somebody else, and what helps others to be saints might ruin him. That is why humility brings with it a deep refinement of spirit, a peacefulness and tact and a common sense without which there is no sane morality.

It is not humility to insist on being someone that you are not. It is as much as saying that you know better than God who you are and who you ought to be. How do you expect to arrive at the end of your own journey if you take the road to another man's city? How do you expect to reach your own perfection by leading somebody else's life? His sanctity will never be yours: you must have the humility to work out your own salvation in a darkness where you are absolutely alone . . . .

And so it takes heroic humility to be yourself and to be nobody but the man, or the artist, that God intended you to be.

From *New Seeds of Contemplation*[8]

We Are One Man

. . . And so one of the worst illusions in the life of contemplation would be to try to find God by barricading yourself inside your own soul, shutting out all external reality by sheer concentration and will-power, cutting yourself off from the world and

other men by stuffing yourself inside your own mind and clos-
ing the door like a turtle.

Fortunately most of the men who try this sort of thing never
succeed. For self-hypnotism is the exact opposite of contemplation. We enter into possession of God when He invades all our
faculties with His light and His infinite fire. We do not "possess"
Him until He takes full possession of us. But this business of
doping your mind and isolating yourself from every thing that
lives, merely deadens you. How can fire take possession of what
is frozen?

The more I become identified with God, the more will I be
identified with all the others who are identified with Him. His
Love will live in all of us. His Spirit will be our One Life, the Life
of all of us and Life of God. And we shall love one another and
God with the same Love with which He loves us and Himself.
This love is God Himself.

From *The Collected Poems of Thomas Merton*[9]

"The Annunciation"

Ashes of paper, ashes of a world
Wandering, when fire is done:
We argue with the drops of rain!

Until One comes Who walks unseen
Even in elements we have destroyed.
Deeper than any nerve
He enters flesh and bone.
Planting His truth, He puts our substance on.
Air, earth and rain
Rework the frame that fire has ruined.
What was dead is waiting for His Flame.
Sparks of His Spirit spend their seeds, and hide
To grow like irises, born before summertime.
These blue things bud in Israel.

The girl prays by the bare wall
Between the lamp and the chair.
(Framed with an angel in our galleries
She has a richer painted room, sometimes a crown.
Yet seven pillars of obscurity

Build her to Wisdom's house, and Ark, and Tower.
She is the Secret of another Testament
She owns their manna in her jar.)

Fifteen years old—
The flowers printed on her dress
Cease moving in the middle of her prayer
When God, Who sends the messenger,
Meets His messenger in her Heart.
Her answer, between breath and breath,
Wrings from her innocence our Sacrament!
In her white body God becomes our Bread.

It is her tenderness
Heats the dead world like David on his bed.
Times that were too soon criminal
And never wanted to be normal
Evade the beast that has pursued
You, me and Adam out of Eden's wood.
Suddenly we find ourselves assembled
Cured and recollected under several green trees.

Her prudence wrestled with the Dove
To hide us in His cloud of steel and silver:
These are the mysteries of her Son.
And here my heart, a purchased outlaw,
Prays in her possession
Until her Jesus makes my heart
Smile like a flower in her blameless hand.

Roger of Taizé
1915–

Roger Louis Schutz-Marsauche is the youngest of nine children of Charles Schutz, a Swiss Protestant pastor, and Amelie Marsauche, the daughter of a French family. The letter from Charles' parents to Amelie's requesting her hand came as a surprise—Amelie had only met him fleetingly at a soirée—but she left Paris and her singing lessons, married, and moved to the Swiss Juras.

Roger was the second son of their nine children; his seven older sisters chose his name. He happily involved himself with the childhood fun in his father's orderly house. It is said they once hid a contraband brood of puppies in the girls' room; found out, the pups were given away. Roger inherited his mother's love of music and his father's love of learning. He listened to recordings of symphonies on the gramophone; with his father's permission he began a "library" at age six.

Roger went to board with a Catholic family at thirteen to be nearer his school. That experience, combined with his maternal grandmother's ecumenical leanings (a Protestant, she still attended, and took communion at, Catholic churches), led him to question the divisions among peoples in the name of Christianity. His uneven recovery from tuberculosis from the ages of seventeen to twenty-one left him a great deal of time to read and prepare himself for a career as a writer and farmer.

He entered his university studies at Strasbourg and Lausanne at twenty-one. Although not particularly drawn to theology, he eventually found within it his life's calling. Yet he clearly did not wish to follow his father's vocation as a pastor. In 1939, his final year of studies at Lausanne, he was invited to be president of the Christian Student Association. During that academic year, Roger's Grand Communauté was born, a sort of third order that met for retreats, reflection and communal prayer. His ideal of community solidified during a retreat with the Carthusians at La Valsainte, where "it was their life of prayer that gripped me."[1]

He returned to his parents' house at the end of his schooling and, while he agreed to return to the Grand Communauté for long weekends, he soon set out to find a place to live his monastic ideal. A combination of coincidences led him to Taizé, then a ruined town half way between Citeaux and Cluny, where he considered buying a house with outbuildings owned by a married couple then living meagerly in Lyon. A neighbor and her daughter offered him a meal, and asked: "Stay here, we are so alone. There is no one left in the village and the winters are so long and cold."[2]

Roger's father agreed with him. This was the cry of the poor, and he must answer it. So for the price of two automobiles he bought the property—on the last day of the owner's novena for its sale. He moved in, set his monastic *horarium,* and began to earn a living. Beyond, he offered refuge for those escaping Nazi rule, for, as be put it, "there was no shortage of people to be hidden and protected."[3] By 1942, the authorities threatened his refuge and him, so he fled to Switzerland, remaining in Geneva for two years. There he continued his thrice-daily monastic prayer in the side chapel of the cathedral together with members of the Grand Communauté, three of whom returned to Taizé with him two years later.

In 1941 he had drafted an 18-page pamphlet describing his concept of a monastic community, essentially *oraret laborea ut regnet:* to pray and to work for the reign of Christ. In 1949 the first seven brothers pronounced permanent vows with Brother Roger as prior; by 1953 twenty received the rule as it had evolved from his first small pamphlet, essentially as it is reproduced below.

Taizé grew as an ecumenical monastic community of men who supported themselves by secular jobs, a challenge to divided Christianity, that gradually became known worldwide by its music and its prior. Brother Roger tirelessly brought the case for Christian unity to the competing centers of Christendom: Canterbury, Constantinople, Geneva, and Rome. He attended every meeting of Vatican II and traveled with Pope Paul VI to Latin America for the International Eucharistic Congress.

Building by building the Taizé property housed more and more Protestant brothers, until 1969 when the first Catholics entered. About one hundred brothers from thirty countries form the Taizé community of today; small fraternities of Taizé monks dot the earth. Brother Roger's intent is not to form a huge monastic community—he accepts very few novices—but, rather, to bring Christian youth together to ecumenical understanding. Most Taizé brothers now work within the community. Their ministry includes "listening" after communal services, which still gather thousands of young people to meetings of prayer and reflection whose aim is commitment in everyday life at home in the parish, school, or workplace. Taizé also organizes "pilgrimages of trust" in cities around the world: Vienna, Johannesburg, Madras, and Paris.

Some have criticized the Taizé concept of Christian unity as naive and dismissive of deep theological differences among denominations, but virtually every denomination shares respect for Brother Roger's revival of the monastic ideal in word, work and music, at Taizé.

From *No Greater Love: Sources of Taizé*

"Sell what you have, give it to the poor, then come, follow me." This challenge of Christ Jesus is one of the most astonishing in the Gospel.

Our vocation as community has committed us to live solely from our work, accepting neither donations nor bequests nor gifts—nothing, absolutely nothing.

The boldness involved in not ensuring any capital for ourselves, without fear of possible poverty, is a source of incalculable strength.

The spirit of poverty does not consist in looking poverty-stricken, but in arranging everything with imagination, in creation's simple beauty.

Happy all who love simplicity: in them is the Kingdom of God.[4]

Christ is communion. Will you choose to live a life rooted not in Christ taken in isolation, but in the Risen Lord present on earth in the communion of his Body, his Church? When the Church is a radiant mystery of motherly love and forgiveness, it offers a clear reflection of Christ Jesus.

One of the earliest witnesses to the Gospel had already grasped this: "Although I might have the gift of speaking in God's name, know all things and have faith strong enough to move mountains, if I do not have love, all that is useless."

In that unique communion which is the Church, oppositions both ancient and new are tearing the Body of Christ apart.

The luminous ecumenical vocation is and always will be a matter of achieving a reconciliation without delay.

For the Gospel, reconciliation does not wait. "When you are bringing your gift to the altar and your sister or brother has something against you, leave everything, first go and be reconciled."

"First go!" Not, "Put off until later."

Ecumenism fosters illusory hopes when it puts off reconciliation till later. It comes to a standstill, becomes fossilized even, when it accepts the creation of parallel paths on which the vital energies of forgiveness are wasted.

Reconciliation makes us fully consistent with the Gospel . . . and so offers a leaven of peace and trust to the entire human family.[5]

Every meal can be a time when brotherly communion finds expression.

At table, times of silence bring peace of heart.

The simplicity of the food reminds us that we have chosen a way that involves sharing with those most in need.[6]

The new brothers need time to mature, in order to understand the vocation in all its consequences.

Certain brothers have been given the responsibility of listening to them and of preparing them for the yes of a whole lifetime.[7]

From *The Life Commitment*

The following words are spoken on the day a brother makes his life commitment in the Taizé Community.

Brother, what do you ask?

The mercy of God and the community of my brothers.

May God complete in you what he has begun.

Brother, you trust in God's mercy: remember that the Lord Christ comes to help the weakness of your faith; committing himself with you, he fulfils for you his promise:

'Truly, there is no one who has given up home, brothers, sisters, mother, father, wife or children for my sake and the Gospel's, who will not receive a hundred times as much at present— homes and brothers and sisters and mothers and children—and persecutions too, and in the age to come eternal life.'

This is a way contrary to all human reason; like Abraham you can only advance along it by faith, not by sight, always sure that whoever loses his life for Christ's sake will find it.

From now on walk in the steps of Christ. Do not be anxious about tomorrow. First seek God's Kingdom and its justice. Surrender yourself, give yourself, and good measure, pressed down, shaken together, brimming over, will be poured out for you; the measure you give is the measure you will receive.

Whether you wake or sleep, night and day the seed springs up and grows, you do not know how.

Avoid parading your goodness before people to gain their admiration. Never let your inner life make you look sad, like a hypocrite who puts on a grief-stricken air to attract attention. Anoint your head and wash your face, so that only your Father who is in secret knows what your heart intends.

Stay simple and full of joy, the joy of the merciful, the joy of brotherly love.

Be vigilant. If you have to rebuke a brother, keep it between the two of you.

Be concerned to establish communion with your neighbour.

Be open about yourself, remembering that you have a brother whose charge it is to listen to you. Bring him your understanding so that he can fulfill his ministry with joy.

The Lord Christ, in his compassion and his love for you, has chosen you to be in the Church a sign of brotherly love. It is his will that with your brothers you live the parable of community. So, refusing to look back, and joyful with infinite gratitude, never fear to rise to meet the dawn,

praising
blessing
and singing
Christ your Lord.

Receive me, Lord, and I will live; may my expectation be a source of joy.

Brother, remember that it is Christ who calls you and that it is to him that you are now going to respond.

Will you, for love of Christ, consecrate yourself to him with all your being?
I will.

Will you henceforth fulfil your service of God within our community, in communion with your brothers?
I will.

Will you, renouncing all ownership, live with your brothers not only in community of material goods but also in community of spiritual goods, striving for openness of heart?
I will.

Will you, in order to be more available to serve with your brothers, and in order to give yourself in undivided love to Christ, remain in celibacy?
I will.

Will you, so that we may be of one heart and one mind and so that the unity of our common service may be fully achieved, adopt the orientations of the community expressed by the prior, bearing in mind that he is only a poor servant in the community?
I will.

Will you, always discerning Christ in your brothers, watch over them in good days and bad, in suffering and in joy?
I will.

In consequence, because of Christ and the Gospel, you are hence-forth a brother of our community.

May this ring be the sign of our fidelity in the Lord.

Words by Brother Roger
© Presses de Taizé
Music: J. S. BACH

Oscar Romero
1917–1980

Oscar Arnulfo Romero y Galdamez was born on August 15, 1917, in the mountain village of Ciudad Barrios, El Salvador. He was apprenticed to a carpenter at age thirteen but shortly thereafter entered the seminary, studied at the Gregorian in Rome, and was ordained there in 1942. He was murdered in the chapel of the Divine Providence Hospital in San Salvador on March 24, 1980, as he concluded his homily in a Mass celebrated for the deceased mother of journalist Jorge Pinto. His last words were of justice.

The sharpshooting thief of justice who murdered the archbishop of San Salvador exercised not the will of the people in his tiny nation on the Pacific Coast of Central America. He exercised the will of the rightist military junta that ruled El Salvador as it suffered the beginnings of an undeclared civil war that eventually took the lives of an estimated seventy-five thousand people before its end in January 1992.

A few years before, in 1975, the government of Colonel Arturo Molina made an initial step toward land reform. By 1976 the government approved a land reform project that would pay for and distribute 150,000 acres of land held by 250 owners to 12,000 *campesino* families. The Salvadoran oligarchy, which owned the majority of the radio stations, and all of the television stations, mounted a major campaign against land reform of any type. President Molina soon dropped the plan, but the concept, supported as it was by the Church, did not die. Luis Chavez, San Salvador's archbishop since 1938, supported the *campesino's* right to political organizing. With increasing regularity, newspapers and radio attacked the Church, and many clerics and religious radically sided with the poor. Then, on reaching age seventy-five, Archbishop Chavez retired.

His replacement on February 22, 1977, was a former auxiliary bishop of San Salvador, by then the bishop of Santiago de Maria, Oscar Romero. Most commentators agree that Romero seemed a safer choice than Auxiliary Bishop Arturo Rivera Damas, who was clearly unpopular with the oligarchy and clearly on the side of the poor. He may well have been, but a single incident radicalized Romero. A Jesuit priest and pastor of the small church at Aguilares, Rutilio Grande, had left his high profile seminary work in 1972 to serve in the poor village where he was born. Grande was a friend of Romero; he had been master of ceremonies in Romero's 1970 ordination as auxiliary bishop. On March 12, 1977, while riding toward Aguilares along the flat rough highway through sugar cane fields, Grande and two others were shot to death.

Romero was outraged, and made his outrage known. It was by then clear that the Salvadoran military was at war with the people. For three years Oscar Romero played a huge role in several facets of that war, refusing to side with the rich or their surrogates. Romero began to speak out after Rutilio Grande's death with an even deeper insistence that human liberation was a gospel right of all. His voice was the voice of the poor and of the voiceless. His eloquence was the eloquence of the heart. His sermons, many of which were broadcast on radio, encouraged the people of El Salvador, caught as they were in the stranglehold of political greed and military power, to believe in their destiny of dignity and justice.

Romero stood, and stands, for the Church persecuted. One of his homilies told of the duty of the Church to be that voice of the voiceless: "This spirit of truth is what gives the Church power to preach, to write, to speak on the radio—to speak the spirit of truth in the face of lies, to undo ambiguities. . . . Persecution is something necessary in the church. Do you know why? Because the truth is always persecuted."[1]

Archbishop Romero came to be roundly criticized, even by some of his own clergy. He lived simply and alone, in a small cottage built for him by the sisters who ran the Divine Providence Hospital, and he often celebrated Mass in the hospital chapel. He also regularly celebrated the 8:00 a.m. Sunday Mass in the archdiocesan cathedral. The revolutionary Gospel he preached in small and large gatherings was the story of Christianity, plain and unvarnished by upper-class pretensions. "To be a Christian now means to have the courage to preach the true teaching of Christ and not be afraid of it, not be silent out of fear and preach something easy that won't cause problems."[2]

It was the poor who came to his Masses. It was the poor who crowded around him in the hamlets he visited. It was the poor who listened to him on the radio. It was the poor whose hearts were shot through when a red car drove up to the Divine Providence Hospital and disgorged a coward with a rifle.

While Archbishop of the Metropolitan See of San Salvador, Oscar Romero wrote four pastoral letters and made formal addresses in the United States and Europe. His consistent message challenged the whole Church to live the possibilities of radical witness to all forms of poverty. That message perdures, especially in El Salvador, where Archbishop Romero is revered as a martyr of and for the poor.

The selections that follow bespeak Oscar Romero the man and the bishop, Oscar Romero the preacher and the pastor. His telephone conversation with José Calderón Salazar, Guatemala correspondent of the Mexican newspaper *Excelsior,* reprinted below, took place about two weeks before his death. The last selection is a translation of his homily on the beatitudes, translated by Ita Ford, a Maryknoll missionary who followed his call for churchworkers to serve in El Salvador and was one of four U.S. churchwomen abducted and killed less than a year after Romero's murder.

November 6, 1977

How I would like to engrave this great idea on each one's heart: Christianity is not a collection of truths to be believed, of laws to be obeyed, of prohibitions. That makes it very distasteful. Christianity is a person, one who loved us so much, one who calls for our love. Christianity is Christ.[3]

From Third Pastoral Letter:
The Church and Popular Political Organizations[4]

The Church at the Service of the People

The second principle that we must lay down is that the church has a mission of service to the people. Precisely from its specifically religious character and mission "come a function, a light, and an energy which can serve to structure and consolidate the human community according to the divine law."*

It is the role of the church to gather into itself all that is human in the people's cause and struggle, above all in the cause of the poor. The church identifies with the poor when they demand their legitimate rights. In our country the right they are demanding is hardly more than the right to survive, to escape from misery.

This solidarity with just aims is not restricted to particular organizations. Whether they call themselves Christian or not, whether they are protected by the government, legally or in practice, or whether they are independent of it and opposed to it, the church is interested only in one thing: if the aim of the struggle is just, the church will support it with all the power of the gospel. In the same way it will denounce, with bold impartiality, all injustice in any organization, wherever it is found. By virtue of this service that it is the church's duty to render, through its faith, to the thirst for justice, it was stated at Medellín that the direction to be taken by pastoral policy in Latin America was "to encourage and favor the efforts of the people to create and develop their own grassroots organizations for the redress and consolidation of their rights and the search for true justice."**

The church is well aware of the complexity of political activity. However, and we repeat it, it is not, nor ought it to be, an expert in this sort of activity. Nevertheless it can and must pass judgment on the general intention and the particular methods of political parties and organizations, precisely because of

---

* *Gaudium et Spes,* §75.
** Medellín, "Peace," §27.

its interest in a more just society. The economic, social, political, and cultural hopes of men and women are not alien to the definitive liberation achieved in Jesus Christ, which is the transcendent hope of the church.*

No less can the church shirk the task of defending the weak and those in real need, whatever the nature of the groups or individuals who support their just causes. As Paul VI remarked:

> It is well known in what terms numerous bishops from all the continents spoke of this at the [1974] synod, especially the bishops from the Third World, with a pastoral accent resonant with the voice of the millions of sons and daughters of the Church who make up those peoples. Peoples, as we know, engaged with all their energy in the effort and struggle to overcome everything which condemns them to remain on the margin of life: famine, chronic disease, illiteracy, poverty, injustices in international relations and especially in commercial exchanges, situations of economic and cultural neo-colonialism sometimes as cruel as the old political colonialism. The Church, as the bishops repeated, has the duty to proclaim the liberation of millions of human beings, many of whom are its own children—the duty of assisting the birth of this liberation, of giving witness to it, of ensuring that it is complete. This is not foreign to evangelization.**

In this service of solidarity with the just causes of the poor, we have not forgotten the duties of the poor themselves and the demands on them to show respect for others. When we have mediated in conflicts, when we have denounced attacks on dignity, life, or liberty, and on other occasions when we have shown this solidarity, we have always tried to be just and objective, and we have never been moved by, nor have we ever preached, hatred or resentment. On the contrary, we have called for conversion. We have pointed to justice as the indispensable basis of the peace that is the true objective of Christians. Among its services to the people the church has performed countless works of charity for the welfare and Christian education of the poor, works that give the lie to those who accuse it of only agitating and never acting.

* See *Evangelii Nuntiandi*, §§29–36.
** Ibid., §30.

The Role of the Struggle for Liberation in Christian Salvation

This is the third principle that, at the theoretical level, guides our reflection on relations between the church and popular organizations. These organizations are forces for the achievement of social, economic, and political justice among the people, especially among the rural poor. The church, as we have said, fosters and encourages just attempts at organization and supports whatever is just in their demands. The church's service to these legitimate efforts for liberation would not, however, be complete if it did not bring to bear on them the light of its faith and its hope, and point out their place in the overall plan of the salvation brought by our Redeemer, Jesus Christ.

The overall plan of the liberation proclaimed by the church:

1) involves the whole person, in all dimensions, including openness to the absolute that is God, and to that extent it is linked to a certain understanding of human nature—an understanding that cannot be sacrificed to the demands of any particular strategy, tactic, or short-term expedient;

2) is centered on the kingdom of God and, although its mission is not limited to religion, it nevertheless reaffirms the primacy of humanity's spiritual vocation and proclaims salvation in Jesus Christ;

3) proceeds from a scriptural vision of human nature, is based on a deep desire for justice in love, implies a truly spiritual dimension that has as its final aim salvation and happiness with God;

4) demands a conversion of heart and mind, and is not satisfied with merely structural changes;

5) and excludes violence, considering it "unchristian and unscriptural," ineffective and out of keeping with the dignity of the people.*

If the church, in its support for any group in its efforts to achieve liberation in this world, were to lose the overall perspective of Christian salvation, "it would lose its fundamental meaning. Its message of liberation would no longer have any originality and would easily be open to monopolization and

---

* See ibid., §§33–37.

manipulation. . . . It would have no more authority to proclaim freedom as in the name of God."*

On the other hand, by cultivating faith and hope in this overall plan of Christ's salvation, the church preaches the real reasons for living, and it puts forward the most solid grounds possible to help persons become aware of themselves as truly free and ready to work with serene confidence for the liberation of the world. Acting in this way the church "is trying more and more to encourage large numbers of Christians to devote themselves to the liberation of men. It is providing these Christian 'liberators' with the inspiration of faith, the motivation of fraternal love, a social teaching which the true Christian cannot ignore and which he must make the foundation of his wisdom and of his experience in order to translate it concretely into forms of action, participation, and commitment."**

To Jose Calderon Salazar, March, 1980

I have often been threatened with death. Nevertheless, as a Christian, I do not believe in death without resurrection. If they kill me, I shall arise in the Salvadoran people. I say so without meaning to boast, with the greatest humility.

As pastor, I am obliged by divine mandate to give my life for those I love—for all Salvadorans, even for those who may be going to kill me. If the threats come to be fulfilled, from this moment I offer my blood to God for the redemption and for the resurrection of El Salvador.

Martyrdom is a grace of God that I do not believe I deserve. But if God accepts the sacrifice of my life, let my blood be a seed of freedom and the sign that hope will soon be reality. Let my death, if it is accepted by God, be for the liberation of my people and as a witness of hope in the future.

You may say, if they succeed in killing me, that I pardon and bless those who do it. Would that thus they might be convinced that they will waste their time. A bishop will die, but the church of God, which is the people, will never perish.[5]

---

* Ibid., §32.
** Ibid., §38.

The Poverties of the Beatitudes[6]

In my thought today I would like to leave this idea: that poverty is a force of liberation because, in addition to being a denouncement of sin & a force of Christian spirituality, it is also a commitment.

These words of Scripture are for me in the first place a [sign] that I should give the example of being Christian—All you dear priests, religious & baptized who call yourselves Christians—listen to what Medellin says: Poverty is a commitment which assumes voluntarily & through love the condition of the needy of this world in order to give testimony to the evil this represents—it also is a spiritual freedom toward goods—following Christ's example who made his own all the consequences of man's sinful condition and who "being rich, became poor" to save us.

The commitment to be a Christian is this: to follow Christ in his incarnation: If it is the majestic God who becomes a man humble unto death on a cross and who lives with the poor, so should be our Christian faith. The Christian who doesn't wish to live the commitment of solidarity with the poor isn't worthy to call himself a Christian.

Christ invites us not to fear persecution because believe me, brothers & sisters, he who is committed to the poor must risk the same fate as the poor.

And in El Salvador we know what the fate of the poor signifies—to disappear, be tortured, to be captive—and be found dead.

He who would want the privileges of this world & not the persecutions of this commitment—fear the tremendous antithesis of today's gospel:

"Happy [are] you, when men hate you & exclude you, insult you & consider you an outcast, for the sake of the son of man. Rejoice & be glad, because your reward will be great in heaven."

Jean Vanier
1928–

Jean Vanier is a son of wealth and privilege who for over thirty years has devoted his life to forming communities with mentally handicapped persons around the world. His privileged state was economic, cultural, and political: Vanier's father was governor-general of Canada. Vanier was educated in England and in Canada, and he served as an officer with both the British and the Canadian Royal Navies.

In 1950 he resigned his commission and moved to France, where he joined "Eau Vive," an international community formed by Dominican Fr. Thomas Philippe (1905–1993) for formation in spirituality, theology, and Christian living. Vanier earned a doctorate in philosophy, writing on Aristotle at the Institut Catholique de Paris. In 1963 Father Philippe became chaplain of the Val Fleuri, a home for thirty mentally handicapped men in Trosly-Breuil, near Compiegne in the north of France.

Vanier's visit changed his life. "My visit moved me very much. Each of the men I met seems starved of friendship and affection: each one clung to me, asking, through words or gestures: 'Do you love me? Do you want to be my friend?' And each one demanded, through his damaged and broken body: 'Why? Why am I like this? Why do my parents not want me? Why can't I be like my brothers and sisters who are married?'"[1]

He began to visit institutions. No matter which—a psychiatric hospital, institution or asylum—each had residents with a common despair. They were unwanted. They knew themselves to be unnecessary to the human community. Yet when they were treated as persons, their faces lit up.

L'Arche was born in August 1964 when Vanier bought a two hundred-year-old farmhouse in Trosley and invited two institutionalized men, Raphael Simi and Philippe Seux, to live there with him and Father Philippe. Each had had meningitis, one could neither talk nor walk; the other could speak but was paralyzed on one side. They had been institutionalized on the death of their parents; neither was asked his preference. Vanier and Philippe formed community with them. Clearly the two handicapped men, and by extension all like them, longed for the fullness of life, for friends who would value them and see them as human.

There are now over four hundred people in that first community in twenty houses spread through five villages in Compiegne. There are two hundred handicapped and two hundred "assistants" as they are called, individuals married or single who live in community and work in gardens and workshops with the others. From Trosly over one hundred other L'Arche communities have grown in twenty-six countries on five continents. All adhere to the same charter and "form a new type of family or community where the strong help the weak, and the weak help the strong."[2]

In addition to residential L'Arche facilities, there are over thirteen hundred Faith and Light communities in seventy countries comprised of people with handicaps, their families and their friends. These non-residential communities meet monthly "to share their sufferings, their joys, to celebrate together and to pray,"[3] also living the L'Arche Charter, which concludes: "L'Arche is deeply concerned by the distress of people who suffer injustice and rejection because they are handicapped. This concern should impel the communities of L'Arche to do all they can do to defend the rights of people with a mental handicap, to support the creation of places of welcome for them and to call our society to become more just and respectful towards them. The communities of L'Arche want to be in solidarity with the poor of the world, and with all those who take part in the struggle for justice."[4]

Jean Vanier's writings are extensive and have one central theme: community. It is community, he says, that humanizes us and lets us understand our worth. It is within community the person grows in love, and that growth is marked by a change from understanding the community as existing for the individual, to the individual existing for the community. Vanier repeatedly points out that community is a difficult project. As he writes, once individuals begin to live in community, they can see their own weaknesses, poverties, disturbances and jealousies. No longer can they exist in an unrealistic bubble believing they love everyone "out there." In community they truly need to learn to love people where they are, right next to them, day in and day out in permanent commitment.

For Vanier, the reality of community, when lived honestly and deeply, is the reality of communion. It is for communion, one with another, that humans were created. "Communion is you are you and I am I and we're called to be in communion together—to be one body. But we've all been wounded in communion . . . I think we all begin with an open heart but then it becomes a wounded heart and then we cover it up."[5]

In 1980 Jean Vanier resigned as day-to-day head of L'Arche, although he still lives in one of its communities: "I hope I can help those who are searching, those who suffer, and those who seek to love."[6]

From *Followers of Jesus*[7]

The Cry for Authenticity

One of the watchwords of our times is "personal relationship", with all the aspects that come from group discussions, sensitivity groups, and group dynamics: "love", "relationship", "dialogue", "communication", "encounter", "I-Thou", "meaningful relationship". These are words which have largely replaced "obedience", "piety", "respect for elders", and the more traditional terminology. These are the key words with young people. They appear in modern literature, and psychology; they are found in the songs of our time. What was important before was that we let ourselves be carried by tradition and all the symbolism of that tradition. Now, it's the encounter, the meeting, the interpersonal relationship that is important. On one side, there is anguish, because of the breakdown of tradition and the life which was so well integrated; on the other side we see rising a thirst, a deep desire for authenticity, for things that are really meaningful based on experience, or at least leading to experience and an interior transformation.

This cry for authenticity goes very deep into one of the aspects of our lives. We want meaningful relationships; we want to meet others at the depths of their beings. We know full well how in religious orders, and in community, we rarely met people on a personal level. We met them on the community level. Personal relationships were, in some ways, suspect because we never knew where they might lead. Now a certain primacy is given to such relationships.

I feel this deeply among the young, who are looking for such encounters, and who quickly get caught up in a world of sexuality, and from there into a world of confusion and sadness. Sometimes in seeking love too quickly, we kill love. Sometimes in wanting a "meeting", an "encounter" at the depths of our being, we stifle the encounter. And then, we doubt the existence of love.

If no communion is possible between two people, then what is left but despair? We have broken down tradition and respect for authority, which gave a certain amount of structure to a person. This breakdown was frequently done in the name of personal relationships and authentic living. And now we wonder whether these relationships are possible, whether truth is possible. Is there really such a thing as love? Maybe "hell is other people" as Sartre says? So what is left but freaking out in the loneliness of drugs, or sinking into the solitude of illusions?

In order to meet someone we have to be true, true in our poverty and in our weakness. But love implies fidelity, fidelity in hardship as in joy. Fidelity means strength of character, an interior force, even a certain discipline. Those who are weak in character can "encounter" in love but they lack the strength to maintain their love. They live an instant of joy but they lack hope, the strength needed to wait and to be patient. This is where tradition can help to prepare one for a life of love. Sometimes in throwing away tradition, we throw away the crutches that would strengthen us and help us to love in joy and in fidelity, in summer and in winter.

In reality this life of openness to the Spirit is a harmony between our growing self, structured by discipline and by effort, and the call, the peace, the joy of the Spirit manifesting Himself to us; it is the harmony between our yearning, our seeking, our fidelity and the answer of His presence; it is also the harmony between sacrifice and communion.

> If any one thirst, let him come to me and drink.
>
> John 7, 37

> If we say we have fellowship with him while we walk in darkness, we lie and do not live according to the truth; but if we walk in the light, as he is in the light, we have fellowship with one another . . .
>
> I John 1, 6-7

> He who loves his brother abides in the light, and in it there is no cause for stumbling.
>
> I John 2, 10

From *Community and Growth*[8]

One Heart, One Soul, One Spirit

In these times, when towns are depersonalised and depersonalising, many people are looking for community, especially when they feel alone, tired, weak and unhappy. Some people find it impossible to be alone; for them, this is a foretaste of death. So community can appear to be a marvellously welcoming and sharing place.

But in another way, community is a terrible place. It is the place where our limitations and our egoism are revealed to us. When we begin to live full-time with others, we discover our poverty and our weaknesses, our inability to get on with people, our mental and emotional blocks, our affective or sexual disturbances, our seemingly insatiable desires, our frustrations and jealousies, our hatred and our wish to destroy. While we were alone, we could believe we loved everyone. Now that we are with others, we realise how incapable we are of loving, how much we deny life to others. And if we become incapable of loving, what is left? There is nothing but blackness, despair and anguish. Love seems an illusion. We seem to be condemned to solitude and death.

So community life brings a painful revelation of our limitations, weaknesses and darkness; the unexpected discovery of the monsters within us is hard to accept. The immediate reaction is to try to destroy the monsters, or to hide them away again, pretending that they don't exist, or to flee from community life and relationships with others, or to find that the monsters are theirs, not ours. But if we accept that the monsters are there, we can let them out and learn to tame them. That is growth towards liberation.

If we are accepted with our limitations as well as our abilities, community gradually becomes a place of liberation. Discovering that we are accepted and loved by others, we are better able to accept and love ourselves. So community is the place where we can be ourselves without fear or constraint. Community life deepens through mutual trust among all its members.

So this terrible place can become one of life and growth. There is nothing more beautiful than a community where people are beginning really to love and trust each other. "Behold, how good and pleasant it is when brothers dwell in unity! It is like the precious oil upon the head, running down upon the beard, upon the beard of Aaron. . . ." (Psalm 133).

I have never understood this reference to Aaron's beard very well—probably because I don't have a beard myself. But if oil running down a beard brings as amazing a feeling as life in community, then it must be marvellous!

* * *

In community life we discover our own deepest wound and learn to accept it. So our rebirth can begin. It is from this very wound that we are born.

* * *

The sense of belonging

When I visit African villages, I realise that through their rituals and traditions they are deeply living community life. Each person has a sense of belonging to the others; men of the same ethnic origin or village are truly brothers. I remember Mgr. Agré, Bishop of Man, meeting a customs officer at Abidjan airport; they embraced like brothers because they came from the same village, they belonged to each other in some way. Most Africans don't need to talk about community. They live it intensely.

I've heard that Aborigines in Australia buy nothing except cars, which enable them to visit their clan. The only thing they find important is this link of brotherhood, which they cherish. There is, it seems, such a unity between them that they know when one of them is dying; they feel it in their guts.

Rene Lenoir, in *Les Exclus*,* says that if a prize is offered for the first to answer a question in a group of Canadian Indian children, they all work out the answer together and shout it out at the same time. They couldn't bear one to win, leaving the rest of them losers. The winner would be separated from his brothers; he would have won the prize but lost solidarity.

Our Western civilization is competitive. From the time they start school, children learn to "win." Their parents are delighted when they come first in class. This is how individualistic material progress and the desire to gain prestige by coming out on top have taken over from the sense of fellowship, compassion and community. Now people live more or less on their own in a small house, jealously guarding their goods and planning to acquire more, with a notice on the gate that says "Beware of the Dog." It is because the West has lost its sense of community that small groups are springing up here and there, trying to refind it.

We have a lot to learn from the African and the Indian. They remind us that the essence of community is a sense of belonging. Of course their sense of community can get in the way of their seeing others objectively and lovingly. That is how tribal wars begin. Sometimes too African community life is based on fear. The group or the tribe give life and a sense of solidarity;

* Le Seuil, Paris 1974.

they protect and offer security, but they are not really liberating. If people cut themselves off from the group, they are alone with their fears and their own deep wound, facing evil forces, wicked spirits and death. These fears are expressed in rites or fetishes, which in turn are a force for cohesion. True community is liberating.

* * *

I love that passage from the Bible: "And I will say . . . 'You are my people'; and he shall say 'Thou art my God'" (Hosea 2,23).

I shall always remember Jessie Jackson, one of Martin Luther King's disciples, saying to a gathering of many thousands of blacks: "My people are humiliated." Mother Theresa of Calcutta says, "My people are hungry."

"My people" are my community, which is both the small community, those who live together, and the larger community which surrounds it and for which it is there. "My people" are those who are written in my flesh as I am in theirs. Whether we are near each other or far away, my brothers and sisters remain written within me. I carry them, and they, me; we know each other again when we meet. To call them "my people" doesn't mean that I feel superior to them, or that I am their shepherd or that I look after them. It means that they are mine as I am theirs. There is a solidarity between us. What touches them, touches me. And when I say "my people", I don't imply that there are others I reject. My people is my community, made up of those who know me and carry me. They are a springboard towards all humanity. I cannot be a universal brother unless I first love my people.

* * *

The longer we journey on the road to unity, the more the sense of belonging grows and deepens. The sense is not just one of belonging to a community. It is a sense of belonging to the universe, to the earth, to the air, to the water, to everything that lives, to all humanity. If the community gives a sense of belonging, it also helps us to accept our aloneness in a personal meeting with God. Through this, the community is open to the universe and to mankind.

* * *

Towards the goals of community

A community must have a project of some kind. If people decide to live together with neither specific goals nor clarity about the "why" of their common life, there will soon be conflicts and the whole thing will collapse. Tensions in community often come from the fact that individuals have not talked about their expectations. They quickly discover that each of them wants something very different. I imagine that the same thing can happen in marriage. It is not simply a question of wanting to live together. If the marriage is to last, you have to know what you want to do and to be together.

This means that every community must have a Charter, which specifies clearly why its members are living together and what is expected of each of them. It also means that before a community begins, its members should take time to prepare for living together and clarify their aims.

Bruno Bettleheim has said:

> "I am convinced communal life can flourish only if it exists for an aim outside itself. Community is viable if it is the outgrowth of a deep involvement in a purpose which is other than, or above, that of being a community."*

The more authentic and creative a community is in its search for the essential, the more its members are called beyond their own concerns and tend to unite. The more lukewarm a community becomes towards its original goals, the more danger there is of its membership crumbling, and of tensions. Its members will no longer talk about how they can best respond to the call of God and the poor. They will talk instead about themselves and their problems, their wealth or their poverty, the structures of the community. There is a vital link between the two poles of community: its goal and the unity of its members.

* * *

A community becomes truly and radiantly one when all its members have a sense of urgency. There are too many people in the world who have no hope. There are too many cries which go unheard. There are too many people dying in loneliness. It is

* *Home for the Heart*, Thames and Hudson, London, 1974.

when the members of a community realise that they are not there simply for themselves or their own sanctification, but to welcome the gift of God, to hasten His Kingdom and to quench the thirst in parched hearts, that they will truly live community. A community must be a light in a world of darkness, a spring of fresh water in the church and for all men. We have no right to become lukewarm.

* * *

From "the community for myself" to "myself for the community"

A community is only a community when the majority of its members is making the transition from "the community for myself" to "myself for the community", when each person's heart is opening to all the others, without any exception. This is the movement from egoism to love, from death to resurrection; it is the Easter, the passover of the Lord. It is also the passing from a land of slavery to a promised land, the land of interior freedom.

A community isn't just a place where people live under the same roof; that is a lodging house or an hotel. Nor is a community a work-team. Even less is it a nest of vipers! It is a place where everyone—or, let's be realistic, the majority!—is emerging from the shadows of egocentricity to the light of a real love.

> "Do nothing from selfishness or conceit, but in humility count others better than yourselves. Let each of you look not only to his own interests, but also to the interests of others."
>
> (Philippians 2,3-4)

Love is neither sentimental nor a passing emotion. It is an attraction to others which gradually becomes commitment, the recognition of a covenant, of a mutual belonging. It is listening to others, being concerned for them and feeling empathy with them. It means answering their call and their deepest needs. It means feeling and suffering with them—weeping when they weep, rejoicing when they rejoice. Loving people means being happy when they are there, sad when they are not. It is living in each other, taking refuge in each other. "Love is a power for unity", says Denys l'Areopage. And if love means moving towards each other, it also and above all means moving together in the same direction, hoping and wishing for the same things. Love means sharing the same vision and the same ideal. So it means wanting others to fulfil themselves, according to God's plan and in service to other people. It means wanting them to be faithful to their own calling, free to love in all the dimensions of their being.

There we have the two poles of community: a sense of belonging to each other and a desire that each of us goes further in our own gift to God and to others, a desire that there is more light in us, and a deeper truth and peace.

> "Love is patient and kind: love is not jealous or boastful; it is not arrogant or rude. Love does not insist on its own way; it is not irritable or resentful; it does not rejoice at wrong, but rejoices in the right. Love bears all things, believes all things, hopes all things, endures all things."
>
> (I Corinthians 13,4-7)

It takes time for a heart to make this passage from egoism to love, from "the community for myself" to "myself for the community", and the community for God and those in need. It takes time and much purification, and constant deaths which bring new resurrections. To love, we must die continually to our own ideas, our own susceptibilities and our own comfort. The path of love is woven of sacrifice. The roots of egoism are deep in our unconscious; our first reactions of self-defence, aggression and the search for personal gratification often grow from them.

Loving is not only a voluntary act which involves controlling and overcoming our own sensibilities—that is just the beginning. It also demands a purified heart and feelings which go out spontaneously to the other. These deep purifications can only come through a gift of God, a grace which springs from the deepest part of ourselves, where the Holy Spirit lives. "I will give them one heart and put a new spirit within them; I will take the stony heart out of their flesh, and give them a heart of flesh" (Ezekiel II;19). Jesus has promised to send us the Holy Spirit, the Paraclete, to infuse us with this new energy, this strength, this quality of heart which will make it possible for us truly to welcome the other—even our enemy—as he or she is, possible for us to bear all things, believe all things, hope all things. Learning to love takes a lifetime, because the Holy Spirit must penetrate even the smallest corners of our being, all the places where there are fears, defences and envy.

Community begins to form when each person tries to welcome and love the others as they are.

"Welcome one another, therefore, as Christ has welcomed you."

(Romans 15,7)

* * *

Sympathies and antipathies

The two great dangers of community are "friends" and "enemies." People very quickly get together with those who are like themselves; we all like to be with someone who pleases us, who shares our ideas, ways of looking at life and sense of humour. We nourish each other, we flatter each other; "You are marvellous"—"So are you"—"We are marvellous because we are intelligent and clever." Human friendships can very quickly become a club of mediocrities, enclosed in mutual flattery and approval. Friendship is then no longer a spur to go further, to be of greater service to our brothers and sisters, to be more faithful to the gifts we have been given, more attentive to the Spirit; we stop walking across the desert to the land of liberation. Friendship becomes stifling, a barrier between ourselves and others and their needs. It can become an emotional dependence which is a form of slavery.

* * *

There are also "antipathies" in community. There are always people with whom we don't agree, who block us, who contradict us and who stifle the treasure of our life and our freedom. Their presence seems menacing and brings out in us either aggression or a sort of servile regression. We seem incapable of expressing ourselves or even of living when we are with them. Others bring out our envy and jealousy; they are everything we wish we were ourselves and their presence reminds us that we are not. Their radiance and their intelligence underline our own poverty. Others ask too much of us: we cannot respond to their incessant emotional demands and we have to push them away. These are the "enemies." They endanger us, and, even if we dare not admit it, we hate them. Certainly, this is only a psychological hatred—it isn't yet a moral hatred, because it is not deliberate. But even so, we just wish these people didn't exist! If they disappeared or died, it would seem like a liberation.

These blocks as well as attractions between different personalities are natural. They come from an emotional immaturity and a whole lot of elements from our childhood over which we have no control. There can be no question of denying them.

But if we let ourselves be guided by our emotional reactions, cliques will very quickly start to form within the community. It will become no longer a community but a collection of people more or less shut in on themselves and blocked off from others. When you go into some communities, you can quickly sense these tensions and underground battles. People don't look each other in the face. They pass each other in the corridors like ships in the night. A community is only a community when the majority of its members have consciously decided to break these barriers and come out of their cocoons of "friendship" to stretch out their hand to their enemies.

But the journey is a long one. A community isn't built in a day. In fact, it is never completely finished. It is always either growing towards greater love, or regressing.

* * *

Our enemies frighten us. We are incapable of hearing their cries, of responding to their needs. Their aggression or domination stifles us. We flee from them—or wish that they would disappear.

In fact, we have to become aware of our own weakness, lack of maturity and inner poverty. Perhaps it is this which we refuse to look at. The faults we criticise in others are often our own which we refuse to face. Those who criticise others and the community, and seek an ideal one, are often in flight from their own flaws and weaknesses. They refuse to accept their own feeling of dissatisfaction, their own wound.

The message of Jesus is clear: "But I say to you that hear, love your enemies, do good to those who hate you, bless those who curse you, pray for those who abuse you. To him who strikes you on the cheek, offer the other also . . . If you love those who love you, what credit is that to you? For even sinners love those who love them" (Luke 6,27–9,32).

* * *

False friends are the ones in whom we see only good qualities. They bring out a vitality and feeling of well-being in us. They reveal us to ourselves and we find them stimulating. That is why we love them. The enemy, by contrast, brings out emotions in us that we don't want to look at: aggression, envy, fear, false dependence, hatred—the whole dark world within us.

As long as we refuse to accept that we are a mixture of light and darkness, of positive qualities and failings, of love and hate, of altruism and egocentricity, of maturity and immaturity, we will continue to divide the world into enemies—the "baddies"—and friends—"the goodies." We will go on throwing up barriers within and around ourselves and spreading prejudice.

When we accept that we have weaknesses and flaws, but that we can still grow towards interior freedom and truer love, then we can accept the weaknesses and flaws of others, who can also grow towards the freedom of love; we can look at all men and women with realism and love. We are all mortal and fragile. But we have a hope, because it is possible to grow.

* * *

Forgiveness at the heart of community

Is it possible, though, to accept ourselves, with our darkness, weaknesses, flaws and fear, without the revelation that God loves us? It is when we discover that the Father sent his only beloved son not to judge us, not to condemn, but to heal, save and guide us on the paths of love, and to forgive us because he loves us in the depths of our being, that we can accept ourselves. There is hope. We are not imprisoned for ever by egoism and darkness. It is possible to love.

So it becomes possible to accept others and to forgive.

* * *

As long as we see in the other only those qualities which reflect our own, no growth is possible; the relationship remains static and sooner or later will end. A relationship is only authentic and stable when it is founded on the acceptance of weakness, on forgiveness and on the hope of growth.

If community reaches its height in celebration, its heart is forgiveness.

* * *

Community is the place of forgiveness. In spite of all the trust we may have in each other, there are always words that wound, self-promoting attitudes, situations where susceptibilities clash. That is why living together implies a certain cross, a constant effort and an acceptance which is daily and mutual forgiveness. Saint Paul says:

> "Put on then, as God's chosen ones, holy and beloved, compassion, kindness, lowliness, meekness and patience, forbearing one another and, if one has a complaint against another, forgiving each other; as the Lord has forgiven you, so you also must forgive. And above all these put on love, which binds everything together in perfect harmony. And let the peace of Christ rule in your hearts, to which indeed you were called in the one body. And be thankful."
>
> (Colossians 3,12-15)

Too many people come into community to find something, to belong to a dynamic group, to find a life which approaches the ideal. If we come into community without knowing that the reason we come is to discover the mystery of forgiveness, we will soon be disappointed.

* * *

Have patience

We are not the masters of our own feelings of attraction or revulsion, which come from the places in ourselves over which we have little or no control. All we can do is try not to follow inclinations which make for barriers within the community. We have to hope that the Holy Spirit will come to forgive, purify and trim the rather twisted branches of our being. Our emotional makeup has grown from a thousand fears and egoisms since our infancy, as well as from signs of love and the gift of God. It is a mixture of shadow and light. And so it will not be straightened out in a day; this will take a thousand purifications and pardons, daily efforts and above all a gift of the Holy Spirit which renews us from within.

* * *

It is a long haul to transform our emotional makeup so that we can start really loving our enemy. We have to be patient with our feelings and fears; we have to be merciful to ourselves. If we are to make the passage to acceptance and love of the other—all the others—we must start very simply, by recognising our own blocks, jealousies, ways of comparing ourselves to others, prejudices and hatreds. We have to recognise that we are poor creatures, that we are what we are. And we have to ask our Father to forgive us. It is good, then, to speak to a priest or a man of God who perhaps could help us to understand what is happening, strengthen us in our efforts and help us discover God's pardon.

Once we have recognised that a branch is twisted, that we have these blocks of antipathy, the next step is to try to be careful of how we speak. We have to try to hold our tongue, which can so quickly sow discord, which likes to spread the faults and mistakes of others, which rejoices when it can prove someone wrong. The tongue is one of the smallest parts of our body, but it can sow death. We are quick to magnify the faults of others, just to hide our own. It is so often "they" who are wrong. When we accept our own flaws, it is easier to accept those of others.

* * *

At the same time, we should try loyally to see the good qualities of our enemies. After all, they must have a few! But because we are afraid of them, perhaps they are afraid of us. If we have blocks, they too must have them. It is hard for two people who are afraid of each other to discover their mutual qualities. They need a mediator, a conciliator, an artisan of peace, someone in whom both have confidence. This third person can perhaps help us to discover the qualities of our enemy, or at least to understand our own attitudes and blocks. When we have seen the enemy's qualities, one day we will be able to use our tongue to say something good about him. It is a long journey, which will end the day we can ask our former "enemy" for advice or a favour. We all find it far more touching to be asked to help than we do to be helped or "done good to."

Throughout this time, the Holy Spirit can help us to pray for our enemies, to pray that they too grow as God would have them grow, so that one day the reconciliation may be made. Perhaps one day the Holy Spirit will liberate us from this block of antipathy. Perhaps He will let us go on walking with this thorn in our flesh—this thorn which humiliates us and forces us to renew our efforts each day. We shouldn't get worried about our bad feelings. Still less should we feel guilty. We should ask God's forgiveness, like little children, and keep on walking. We shouldn't get discouraged if the road is long. One of the roles of community life is precisely to keep us walking in hope, to help us accept ourselves as we are and others as they are.

Patience, like forgiveness, is at the heart of community life—patience with ourselves and the laws of our own growth, and patience with others. The hope of a community is founded on the acceptance and love of ourselves and others as we really are, and on the patience and trust which is essential to growth.

* * *

Mutual trust

The mutual trust at the heart of community is born of each day's forgiveness and the acceptance of our frailty and poverty. But this trust is not developed overnight. That is why it takes time to form a real community. When people join a community, they always present a certain image of themselves because they want to conform to what the others expect of them. Gradually, they discover that the others love them as they are and trust them. But this trust must stand the test and must always be growing.

Newly-married couples may love each other a great deal. But there may be something superficial in this love, which has to do with the excitement of discovery. Love is even deeper between people who have been married for a long time, who have lived through difficulties together and who know that the other will be faithful until death. They know that nothing can break their union.

It is the same in our communities. It is often after suffering, after very great trials, tensions and the proof of fidelity that trust grows. A community in which there is truly mutual trust is a community which is indestructable.

* * *

So a community is not simply a group of people who love to-gether and love each other. It is a current of life, a heart, a soul, a spirit. It is people who love each other a great deal and who are all reaching towards the same hope. This is what brings the special atmosphere of joy and welcome which characterises the true community.

> "So if there is any encouragement in Christ, any incentive of love, any participation in the Spirit, any affection and sympathy, complete my joy by being of the same mind, having the same love, being in full accord and of one mind."
>
> (Philippians 2,1-2)

> "Now the company of those who believed were of one heart and soul, and no one said that any of the things which he possessed was his own, but they had every thing in common."
>
> (Acts 4,32)

This atmosphere of joy comes from the fact that we all feel free to be ourselves in the deepest sense. We have no need to play a role, to pretend to be better than the others, to demonstrate prowess in order to be loved. We have discovered that we are loved for ourselves, not for our intellectual or manual skills.

When we begin to drop the barriers and fears which prevent us from being ourselves, we become more simple. Simplicity is no more and no less than being ourselves. It is knowing that we are accepted with our qualities, our flaws and as we most deeply are.

* * *

I am becoming more and more aware that the great difficulty of many of us who live in community is that we lack self-confidence. We can so quickly feel that we are not really loveable, that if others saw us as we really were, they would reject us. We are afraid to face our emotional or sexual problems; we are afraid that we are incapable of real love. We swing so quickly from exhilaration to depression, and neither expresses what we really are. How can we become convinced that we are loved in our poverty and weakness and that we too are capable of loving?

That is the secret of growth in community. It comes from a gift of God which may pass through others. As we discover gradually that God and the others trust us, it becomes a little easier for us to trust ourselves, and in turn to trust others.

* * *

To live in community is to discover and love the secret of what is unique in ourselves. This is how we become free. Then we no longer live according to the desires of others, or by an image of ourselves; we become free to discover the essence of the other.

* * *

The right to be oneself

I have always wanted to write a book called *The Right to be a Rotter*. A fairer title is perhaps, *The Right to be Oneself*. One of the great difficulties of community life is that we sometimes force people to be what they are not: we stick an ideal image on them to which they are obliged to conform. If they don't manage to live up to this image, they become afraid that they won't be loved, or that they will disappoint others. If they do live up to the image, then they think they are perfect. But community is not about perfect people. It is about people who are bound to each other, each of whom is their own mixture of good and bad, darkness and light, love and hate. And community is the only earth in which each of them can grow without fear towards the liberation of the forces of love which are hidden in them. But there can only be growth if we recognise the potential; and so there are many things in us to be purified—there are shadows to turn into light and fears to turn into trust.

Often we expect too much of people in community life. We prevent them from discovering and accepting themselves as they are. We are so quick to judge them or to put them into categories. So they feel obliged to hide behind a mask. But they have the right to be rotters, to have their own dark places, and corners of envy and even hatred in their hearts. These jealousies and insecurities are natural; they aren't any kind of "shameful disease." They are part of our wounded nature. That is our reality. We have to learn to accept them and to live with them without drama, and to walk towards liberation, gradually knowing ourselves to be forgiven.

Some people in community, it seems to me, live a sort of unconscious guilt; they feel that they are not what they should be. They need to be affirmed and encouraged to trust. They must feel able to share even their weaknesses without the risk of rejection.

* * *

There is a part of each of us which is already luminous, already converted. And there is a part which is still in shadow. A community is not made up only of the converted. It is made up of all the elements in us which need to be transformed, purified and pruned. It is made up also of the "unconverted."

* * *

There are people in community with very deep psychological wounds, who carry real blocks and serious neuroses. They were terribly bruised in their childhood; they have had to build huge barriers because of their vulnerability. They don't always need to be sent to a psychiatrist, nor to be given psychotherapy. Many people are called to live all their lives with these blocks and barriers. They too are children of God and God can work through and with them, and with their neuroses, for the good of the community. They too have their gift to offer. Don't let's "psychiatrise" things too much. Through the forgiveness of each day, let us help each other to accept these neuroses and barriers.

Anyway, that's the best way to dissolve them!

* * *

Called together just as we are

God seems pleased to call together in Christian communities people who, humanly speaking, are very different, who come from very different cultures, classes and countries. The most beautiful communities are created from just this diversity of people and temperaments. This means that each person must love the others with all their differences, and work with them for the community.

These people would never have chosen to live with each other. Humanly speaking, it seems an impossible challenge. But it is precisely because it is impossible that they have an inner conviction that God has chosen them to live in this community. And so the impossible becomes possible. They no longer rely on their own human abilities or natural sympathies, but on their Father who has called them to live together. He will give them the new heart and spirit which will enable them all to become witnesses to love. In fact, the more impossible it is in human terms, the more of a sign it is that their love comes from God and that Jesus is living: "By this all men will know that you are my disciples, if you have love for one another" (John 13,35).

* * *

When he created the first community of the apostles, Jesus chose to live with men who were very different from one another: Peter, Matthew (the publican), Simon (the Zealot), Judas, and so on. They would never have come together if their Master had not called them.

* * *

We shouldn't seek the ideal community. It is a question of loving those whom God has set beside us today. They are signs of God. We might have chosen different people, people who were more cheerful and intelligent. But these are the ones God has given us, the ones He has chosen for us. It is with them that we are called to create unity and live a covenant.

* * *

I am more and more struck by people in community who are dissatisfied. When they live in small communities, they want to be in larger ones, where there is more nourishment, where there are more community activities, or where the liturgy is more beautifully prepared. And when they are in large communities, they dream of ideal small ones. Those who have a lot to do dream of having plenty of time for prayer; those who have a lot of time for themselves seem to get bored and search distractedly for some sort of activity which will give a sense to their lives. And don't we all dream of the perfect community, where we will be at peace and in complete harmony, with a perfect balance between the exterior and the interior, where everything will be joyful?

It is difficult to make people understand that the ideal doesn't exist, that personal equilibrium and the harmony they dream of come only after years and years of struggle, and that even then they come only as flashes of grace and peace. If we are always looking for our own equilibrium, I'd even say if we are looking too much for our own peace, we will never find it, because peace is the fruit of love and service to others. I'd like to tell the many people in communities who are looking for this impossible ideal: "Stop looking for peace, give yourselves where you are. Stop looking at yourselves—look instead at your brothers and sisters in need. Be close to those God has given you in community today; work with the references which God has given you today. Ask how you can better love your brothers and sisters. Then you will find peace. You will find rest and that famous balance you're looking for between the exterior and the interior, between prayer and activity, between time for yourself and time for others. Everything will resolve itself through love. Stop wasting time running after the perfect community. Live your life fully in your community today. Stop seeing the flaws— and thank God there are some! Look rather at your own defects and know that you are forgiven and can, in your turn, forgive others and today enter into the conversion of love."

* * *

Sometimes it is easier to hear the cries of poor people who are far away than it is to hear the cries of your brothers and sisters in your community. There is nothing very splendid about responding to the cry of the person who is with you day after day and who gets on your nerves. Perhaps we can only respond to the cries of others when we have recognised and assumed the cry of our own wound.

* * *

Share your weakness

The other day, Colleen, who has been living in community for more than twenty-five years, told me: "I have always wanted to be transparent in community life. I have wanted more than anything to avoid being an obstacle to God's love for the others. Now I am beginning to discover that I am an obstacle and I always shall be. But isn't the recognition that I am an obstacle, sharing that with my brothers and sisters and asking their forgiveness, what community life is all about?" There is no ideal community. Any community is made up of people with all their richness, but also with their weakness and their poverty, of people who accept and forgive each other. Humility and trust are more at the foundation of community life than perfection and devotion.

* * *

To accept our weaknesses and those of others is the very opposite of sloppy complacency. It is not a fatalistic and hopeless acceptance. It is essentially a concern for truth, so that we do not live in illusion and can grow from where we are and not where we want to be, or where others want us to be. It is only when we are conscious of who we are and who the others are, with all our wealth and weakness, and when we are conscious of the call of God and the life He gives us, that we can build something together. The force for life should spring from the reality of who we are.

* * *

The more a community deepens, the weaker and the more sensitive its members become. You might think exactly the opposite—that as their trust in each other grows, they in fact grow stronger. So they do. But this doesn't dispel the fragility and sensitivity which are at the root of a new grace and which mean that people are becoming in some way dependent on each other. Love makes us weak and vulnerable, because it breaks down the barriers and protective armour we have built around ourselves. Love means letting others reach us and becoming sensitive enough to reach them. The cement of unity is interdependence.

* * *

Didier expressed this in his own way during a community meeting: "A community is built like a house, with all sorts of different materials. Cement holds the stones together. And cement is made of sand and lime, which are very insubstantial— it takes only a gust of wind to blow them away in a cloud of dust. The cement that unites us in our community is the part of us that is weakest and smallest."

* * *

Community is made of the gentle concern that people show each other every day. It is made of small gestures, of services and sacrifices which say "I love you" and "I'm happy to be with you." It is letting the other go in front of you, not trying to prove that you are right in a discussion; it is taking small burdens from the other.

* * *

If living in community means letting down the barriers which protect our vulnerability and recognising and welcoming our weakness, and so growing, then people who are separated from their community are bound to feel terribly vulnerable. Those who live all the time in the struggles of society have to build an armour around their vulnerability.

People who have spent a long time at l'Arche sometimes discover a whole lot of aggression in themselves when they return to their family, which they find very hard to bear. They had thought that this aggression no longer existed. So they begin to doubt their calling and who they really are. But the aggression is to be expected, because they have been stripped of much of their personal armour in community. But they cannot live so openly with people who do not respect their vulnerability. They have to defend themselves.

* * *

From *From Brokenness to Community*[9]

When I was in the navy, I was taught to give orders to others. That came quite naturally to me! All my life I had been taught to climb the ladder, to seek promotion, to compete, to be the best, to win prizes. This is what society teaches us. In doing so, we lose community and communion. It was not natural or easy for me to live in communion with people, just to be with them. How much more difficult it was for me to be in communion with people who could hardly speak or had little to speak about.

Communion did not come easily to me. I had to change and to change quite radically. When you have been taught from an early age to be first, to win, and then suddenly you sense that you are being called by Jesus to go down the ladder and to share your life with those who have little culture, who are poor and marginalized, a real struggle breaks out within oneself. As I began living with people like Raphael and Philip, I began to see all the hardness of my heart. It is painful to discover the hardness in one's own heart. Raphael and the others were crying out simply for friendship and I did not quite know how to respond because of the other forces within me, pulling me to go up the ladder.

But over the years, the people I live with in L'Arche have been teaching and healing me.

They have been teaching me that behind the need for me to win, there are my own fears and anguish, the fear of being devalued or pushed aside, the fear of opening up my heart and of being vulnerable or of feeling helpless in front of others in pain; there is the pain and brokenness of my own heart.

I discovered something which I had never confronted before, that there were immense forces of darkness and hatred within my own heart. At particular moments of fatigue or stress, I saw forces of hate rising up inside me, and the capacity to hurt someone who was weak and was provoking me! That, I think, was what caused me the most pain: to discover who I really am, and to realize that maybe I did not want to know who I really was! I did not want to admit all the garbage inside me. And then I had to decide whether I would just continue to pretend that I was okay and throw myself into hyperactivity, projects where I could forget all the garbage and prove to others how good I was. Elitism is the sickness of us all. We all want to be on the winning team. That is at the heart of apartheid and every form of racism. The important thing is to become conscious of those forces in us and to work at being liberated from them and to discover that the worst enemy is inside our own hearts not outside!

Thea Bowman
1937–1990

The simple statistics of her life do not encompass the enormous magnetic appeal of Thea Bowman, whose words and music are but glimpses into the depths of her apostolic spirituality.

Thea Bowman was born Bertha Bowman in Yazoo City, Mississippi. Her parents, Mary Esther Coleman, a teacher, and Theon Edward Bowman, a doctor, had no other children. When she was ten, Thea was baptized and received into the Catholic Church; when she was twelve her mother transferred her to a new Catholic school, run by the Franciscan Sisters of Perpetual Adoration.

In 1953 she entered the Franciscan Sisters community in LaCrosse, Wisconsin. Before she entered their novitiate, however, she contracted tuberculosis, and spent a year at River Pines Sanitarium in Stevens Point, Wisconsin (coincidentally, the same sanitarium where Jessica Powers spent twelve months a few years later).

At twenty-one, after first vows, she began teaching in LaCrosse. She later taught in Canton, Mississippi. In 1968 she began graduate studies in English at The Catholic University of America in Washington, D.C., and received the doctorate in 1972. For six years she taught at the Franciscan Sisters' Viterbo College, until she returned to Canton to care for her elderly parents. While in Canton, she began working with the Office of Intercultural Awareness for the Diocese of Jackson, Mississippi, and became increasingly popular as a speaker. She was a founding faculty member and served at the Institute of Black Catholic Studies at Xavier University in New Orleans, Louisiana, from 1980 to 1989.

In 1984, the same year both her parents died, Thea was diagnosed with breast cancer. Her explosion of joy, at being black and being Catholic, was just being noticed. In 1985, she visited Africa, and attended the Forty-third International Eucharistic Congress in Nairobi. Her determined living in the present attracted more attention. She received the Harriet Tubman Award from the National Black Sisters' Conference. She spoke to more and larger groups. By 1987, CBS' "Sixty Minutes" ran a segment about her. She was choosing life, and challenging everyone to choose along with her.

Thea Bowman did not write so much as she spoke and sang the Gospel. Much of her work is preserved on audio and videotapes. In 1987 she delivered the talk "Cosmic Spirituality: No Neutral Ground" to the Religious Formation Conference, the membership group of men and women charged by their religious orders with accepting and training new candidates for religious life. "Cosmic Spirituality" was the theme they chose; she quickly challenged their own cosmic initiative. "The majority of the people in the Catholic Church," she reminded them, "are people of color."[1] And yet the majority of religious in the United States, if not the world, are not people of color. What happens, she asks, when people with non-European roots come to religious congregations? What happens when people who dare to challenge come to religious congregations? What happens to people who are different, in one way or another, from the communities into which they seek to be inculturated? What, she asks by implication, happens to the Church when it merely seems to replicate itself?

Thea Bowman died on March 30, 1990, in Canton, Mississippi. A few months later she became the first and only posthumous recipient of the Laetare Medal of the University of Notre Dame. Since then, programs, schools, and centers named for her honor her infectious delight in having been made in the image and likeness of God.

From *No Neutral Ground* (Cana text: John 2:1-11)

SISTER THEA BOWMAN: Let us pray. *(Singing)*

The Religious Formation Conference sings of peace in New Orleans at the Clarion Hotel, 15 Canal Street. Neutral ground is just outside the door and the Iberville Project is just across the street. The Clarion Hotel and the Iberville Project, affluence and poverty, with only neutral ground between.

You sing of peace on neutral ground. The Indians were here. Still in 1682 La Salle claimed Louisiana for the Sun King, Louis Quattorze. Jean Baptiste LeMans, DeBienville, established a settlement, this tiny town called Novelle Orleans. Despite papal prohibition he introduced slavery into the whole territory and established the infamous Black Codes. Then 88 women set free from Paris prisons came over to be brides for the settlers. They were chaperoned by eight Ursuline nuns.

In 1726, legend tells us, Louis XV lost a bet and gave Charles III of Spain the whole Louisiana Territory in payment. When Spain ran out of money during the war with Britain, they sold the Louisiana back to France. Then in 1803 when Napoleon needed money, he sold the Louisiana Territory to the Americans for $15 million. Are you with me, Church?

South of Canal Street was the French Quarter, where French and Spanish Catholics lived. North of the canal the British came in with the cotton industry and big money to create what they called a "higher strata of society." The Americans came in as new citizens. They were regarded with great disdain by the Creoles and New Orleanians. Unwelcomed in the French Quarter, the new arrivals began building their fine homes on the other side of what was intended to be a drainage canal. And the fighting started.

The original purpose of the Canal Street neutral ground was to keep the French-Spanish Catholic people from fighting with the British-American Protestant folks. Canal Street was neutral ground. Today I suppose you would call it the "demilitarized zone." Neutral ground was designed to separate cultures in conflict.

It is cultural variety, however, that gives New Orleans its richness and breadth, its beauty, texture and flavor. The heritage, culture, tradition, the expression, arts and values of Choctaw Indians, French trader settlers, Arcadians, Cajuns, black slaves who were field workers but also builders, iron artists and nurturers of children—Creoles, Spaniards and West Indians, travelers and tourists, businesspeople flying ships from many nations and ports and bringing people here from all over the world. The French Quarter, the Vieux Carre, Jackson Square, the Cathedral, the Cavildo, Italianate courtyards, Spanish colonades, early American mansions, next to Pat O'Brien's, Preservation Hall. Shrimp and crawfish, filet gumbo, Dookey's, feasting and festival; wine, women, song, dance and romance. Mardi Gras, fifty-five parades, a conservative estimate, hundreds of floats, thousands of New Orleanians and their guests having a festival time. What a fitting place to celebrate the wedding feast of Cana.

There follows a dramatization of the Wedding Feast of Cana with song, dance, dialogue and gesture in Black New Orleanian style.

NARRATOR: *There was, on the third day, a wedding feast at Cana. (Music)*

On the third day, there was a wedding at Cana in Galilee, and the mother of Jesus was there. Jesus and his disciples had been invited likewise to the celebration. At a certain point, the wine ran out. The mother of Jesus told him:

MARY: *Son, son, they have no more wine. Do something.*

JESUS: *What concern is that of mine? Why do you bring this concern to me? My hour has not yet come.*

NARRATOR: *His mother instructed those waiting on the table.*

MARY: *Waiter, waiter. Waiter, waiter. Do whatever he tells you.*

NARRATOR: *As prescribed for Jewish ceremonial washings, there were at hand six stone water jars, each one holding 15 to 25 gallons.*

JESUS: *Fill those jugs with water.*

NARRATOR: *Jesus ordered. At which they filled them to the brim.*

JESUS: *Now take that to the chief steward.*

NARRATOR: *They did as he instructed. The steward tasted the water made wine without knowing where it had come from. Only the waiters knew, since they had drawn the water. Then the steward called the groom over and remarked to him:*

CHIEF STEWARD: *Look at them legs on that glass. Man, this is some bad stuff. You know usually when you have a wedding and you have guests over, you serve the best wine first, but man, you dirty dog, you done saved the best till the last. Man. This is all right!!*

NARRATOR: *Jesus performed this first of his signs in Cana in Galilee. Thus did he reveal his glory and his disciples believed in him. (Music)*

You are formation personnel. Your conference theme is cosmic spirituality. We think you're talking about the spirituality of the cosmos, the spirituality of the universe. You are helping men and women prepare themselves for life and ministry in a multicultural Church and world. You're trying to help folks get in touch with the spirituality that is of us all. The majority of people in the Catholic church are not white, European, Caucasian. The majority of people in the Catholic church are people of color. The majority of the people in the world are people of color. And it's the cosmos, the universe, the world in all its diversity spirituality for which we are preparing ourselves and our congregations. Cosmic spirituality means we're going to have to learn new languages. We're going to have to learn new rhythm. We're going to have to learn new ways of glorifying the Lord. How can you teach your folks back home if you can't share a culture and spirituality that's different and unfamiliar. You can't learn culture or spirituality by reading a book. If you could, we'd all be better informed. We learn cultures and customs and languages of faith, we learn cosmic spirituality by *sharing,* by sharing prayer and song and ritual and story, by involving ourselves and participating, by giving and receiving.

So I'm urging you to urge the people at your table to engage themselves. Sing, pray, work with us. We didn't come here to entertain or perform. We came to share our faith and our spirituality with you. We are working ourselves down trying to help you understand. It's New Orleans, in the South, and black folk are working hard to share faith and life with you, to share spirituality with you. Are you just going to sit there? Is that what you had in mind?

I hope this isn't on the videotape, but this is serious. We invite men and women from the cultures of the world to come into our congregations. Men and women with roots in Asia, Africa, Australia, Latin America, Native America and the Islands. We invite them. They come from New Orleans or Canton, Mississippi, from Haiti or the Iroquois Reservation, from Mexico or El Salvador or the Philippines, from China, India, Vietnam, Nigeria or Harlem. So often in formation and in community their spiritual gifts and spiritual journies are dismissed or ignored. Talk with the people of color in your congregations, in your formation programs. Ask them to what extent they believe that you are serious about understanding them—their history, their experience, their culture, their heritage, their art, their music, their styles of prayer, their styles of meeting, their songs, their dances, their modalities of relationship. To what extent are you serious about sharing their spirituality, their styles of life and prayer and relationship? Ask them how they feel in your congregation. Have you asked them lately?

When Jesus is among us, to work among us miracles of transformation and miracles of love, there is no neutral ground. Neutral ground becomes loving ground; loving ground becomes holy ground; holy ground becomes kingdom ground. We are the children of the cosmos, the children of the universe. In this world of rapid transit; supersonic, interplanetary, sonar communication; computerized nuclear technology, robotics, some folk go to Europe, Australia and Africa like we used to go to New Orleans and Chicago. We're children of the universe, called and sent to transform the cosmos.

Jesus is able. We believe he is a Waymaker, and when we come together in Jesus' name, we come for transformation. Cosmic spirituality means we come together, bring our gifts, bringing our histories, bringing our experience, bringing our positives and negatives, our arts, our skills, our teaching-learning methodologies—all of them—all that we have and all that we hold. Bearing and wearing our best, we come to the Wedding Feast and we do as Jesus said, we draw the water. We carry it to the chief steward and we testify to the miracle.

We become the miracle when we love one another. God so loved the world that he gave his only begotten son so that whosoever believeth in Him would not perish but would have everlasting life. And Jesus says to us, "As the Father has loved me, love one another." Now how can you love somebody you don't know? And how will you know if you do not study, if you do not sit at the feet of the elders, if you do not learn from the little children, if you do not read the books and see the plays and hear the music? How can you prepare for a world that's cosmic? How can you share a spirituality that shares Gospel values within the cosmos?

Jesus says, "As the Father loves me, I love you." And "As I have loved you, love one another."

He doesn't say love anyone that looks like you, thinks like you, prays like you, dresses like you, talks like you. "Love one another as I have loved you. Greater love than this nobody has than to lay down life." You try to work with us sometime. You get tired of us. You get discouraged with us. I remember when you were talking about going where you had never have been before. You remember those days? Uh huh. And some of those folk who went where they had never been before never found themselves at home where they had never been before. They decided to go back home. That was a good idea.

Jesus said, "They will know that you are mine, because you love one another." When we love one another, we become the miracle. We witness to the miracle. We are transformed by His love and the world beholds his glory in our transformation. Are you with me, Church?

Cana mother said to Son, "They have no wine."
Cana mother said to them, "Do whatever he tells you,"
And the water became purest wine.
And wine became his precious blood.
Cana mother says to Son, "Son, they are not free.
Son, they are oppressed.
Son, they yearn for peace that they have not known.
Son, they are unemployed.
Son, they are indigent and they have not the means to learn and to help themselves.
Son, they are alienated in a world that is oppressive, exploitive and cold."
Cana mother says to Son.
Son says to waiters.
Son says to servants.
Son says to ministers,
"Go to their wells and bring the water."
Jesus didn't say to go out there and fix it. "Bring the water to me." Bring it to Jesus, that's all we have to do.

I was really surprised when I found out that the Religious Formation Conference was concentrating its attention on a wedding feast. I was really surprised, weren't you surprised? I mean times sure have changed.

Wedding Feast—the underlying sensuality and sexuality; the emphasis on procreation and progeny; the inner turmoil that has to do with change and risk and newness and relationship; the emphasis on exclusiveness in friendship and in love; the financial conflicts.

Jesus did something with that wine. Look really seriously at the recipe; six wine pots and each holding two or three measures. We are talking about 130 to 180 gallons of wine. If a virgin married in Jewish times, the party lasted one week, a seven day feast, serious party, an abundance of wine.

Mary noticed that they were running out of wine. "They didn't need that wine," some of you would have said. "These people are poor," some of you would have said. "The emphasis on wealth, abundance, prosperity and spending is totally out of order." Isn't that what you would have said?

But Jesus understood the cultural modality. The abundance of wine was a symbol of hospitality and graciousness. It symbolized the promise of prosperity and generosity. The failure of wine symbolized inadequacy and deficiency, embarrassment and shame, inability to provide that which was required. The singing and the dancing and the breaking of the glass, the feasting and the festivity could not proceed without the abundance of wine. And Jesus understood. Are you with me, Church?

Think how long those poor folks had been saving for a celebration that lasted a whole week. Jesus understood. And in the neutral ground that became kingdom ground, that became loving ground, miracles were worked. Jesus used *their* water. He used *their* pots. He *used* their waiters. He used their chief steward. His mama was one of them. And you know what they said about him, "Isn't that Joseph's son? Isn't that the carpenter's son?"

Jesus respected who they were and how they were. And therefore, neutral ground became loving ground, became holy ground, became kingdom ground. Holy.

So you all sit and look. You sit out there and look. I'm talking culture. I'm black, y'all. And proud. And this is New Orleans, y'all. Do you know how to shout *"hallelujah," "thank you Jesus."*

Formation, transformation. Come to the wedding feast with awareness and with compassion. Let Jesus instruct you. Let the waiters draw the water. Let them fill the jars. Let the stewards taste and testify. Your words don't mean that much. You're going home. Let Jesus reveal his glory and his disciples will believe. Jesus changed water into wine of finest quality. Some of you would have thought that was too fine for those people. Well, yeah. We're talking about cosmic spirituality. We're talking about the independence and the interdependence of all the world's people. And if we take the Cana story seriously, we will be rocketed and ricocheted out of our old complacencies. Off neutral ground and onto kingdom ground.

Jesus said to his mama his hour had not come. You know how we are. We sit around and wait for the hour. But Mary by her belief, by her faith, by her persistence, could call upon her Son. "The modest waters saw their God, and blushed." Jesus revealed his glory.

When you come into my community, my town, my world, will you see God's glory revealed? When you go to my brothers and sisters, in beautiful Hawaii, will you see his glory? When you experience, when you share the hungers of Ethiopia, the blood flow of Guatemala and Nicaragua, will you see his glory revealed?

I want to take you way back. "Gimme that old time religion." I have to praise the Lord the way I know how to praise the Lord. And as I bless his holy name, are you prepared to learn from me, in your formation program.

You say, "Lord, teach us to pray." You taught me to pray. Are you ready to learn from me? You teach the people who come to you in formation. Do you learn from them the habits of prayer that they bring from their homes, from their cultures? Or do you try to remake them according to your mold and fashion? Do we come together to share bread, to share prayer, to *share* styles and modalities of faith and worship? Or do we always have to do things your way?

If I always have to come into your house and be a stranger, I might as well go home to my mama, or my daddy, my community, where they know me and love me. I'm talking about seminarians. I'm talking about young women in formation who enter congregations where they don't find home. If you know what I'm talking about, say *Amen.*

I'm talking about my friend Marcy who said she never really felt like she prayed unless she prayed in Spanish because her grandmothers and her aunts and her mother and her father taught her how to pray in Spanish. *(Music)*

If you believe that the spirit that lived in Jesus, that the spirit that lived in the disciples, that the spirit that moved in the early church is the same spirit you receive in your baptism and confirmation, say *Amen.* If you believe that you like Jesus, are called by the spirit to share the spirit in the world to call forth the giftedness of God's people, say *Amen.* If you believe that God is able to work in all the brothers and the sisters, in the ones you customarily write off because they don't read right, they don't write right, they drink too much, they smoke the wrong thing, they don't walk right, they don't talk right, their sexual preferences are not in agreement with the ones you claim.

If you believe that God is able to transform the water of my reality into purest wine, if you believe there's nothing God can't do, let me hear you say *Amen. (Music)* . . . .

The goal of the system, the black community and the candidate, are essentially the same: to recruit, maintain, sustain black candidates so that the Church may grow from the service of such individuals. Now, I'm talking to you about the black community and I'm talking to you about black candidates, but there are those among you who can talk to you about the needs of the Native American or the Hispanic or the Asian.

In this cosmic system where we find ourselves, Jesus calls red, black, white, brown, yellow and all the hues and colors between, the children of all Africa and Asia, and Central America and the Islands, and Europe and North America. Jesus calls. He calls the young and the middle aged and the geriatric generation too. We come together in this cosmic society needing love and security and nurturance and stability. Single, married, divorced, folks from non-functional families. Communities used to deny the problems.

Only virgins of good reputation and good family were admitted. Now Jesus calls virgins of good repute, also victims of sexual abuse, child abuse, chemical abuse, violence and war; some who have been and perhaps are sexually, heterosexually, homosexually active, presenting the whole threat of AIDS in our formation programs; some people who are sexually preoccupied, misunderstood, misunderstanding, and grieving. Jesus calls college graduates, competent, experienced, effective, multi-degreed, traveled, professionals, politicians, educators, administrators, health care professionals. It's a cosmic world. Jesus calls to the diverse, and how often they find themselves misunderstood.

All my life my momma told me to stand up straight, hold up my head and speak out. And what happens to the person in formation who dares to? We have the children among us of alienation and anger and frustration, of guilt and shame, men and women with unexpressed hopes and loves and yearnings, with feelings of separation and denial. Children of the universe we come together in Jesus' Name and the only answer that we can offer to one another is the love that is found in the word of God, the love that is shared and celebrated in Jesus' Name. Love, enunciated in a thousand languages, a thousand symbols, a thousand rituals, a thousand ways so that the giftedness and the heritage of the multiplicity of God's people becomes available to all of us and to the Church that we call our home. *(Music)*

We blacks at the Clarion Hotel in New Orleans offer to share with you a style of contemplation, a modality of prayer. We attempt to reach out and to establish community with you. We try to teach you about ourselves, our ways, our culture. Do you experience a reticence, a holding back, an unwillingness to risk trying to share our lives, our prayers, our style of communication and teaching? Tired people who have worked all day, cripples and pregnant women are over-extending themselves in an effort to reach you, to involve you, to wake you up, to share our spirituality, our spiritual gifts with you. How have you responded? More importantly what happens when candidates or persons of color enter your congregation? We go to prayer service, and you hand us five typed sheets. We read. Our folks have taught us from babyhood, "Praise the Lord with your whole heart, and your whole soul and your whole mind and all your strength, wholistically." They have been taught to bring memory and imagination and feeling and passion and emotion to prayer, to use the whole body in praise of the Lord. The way of black folk in prayer is the way of total engagement.

When I come into your congregation with you, when I come into your formation program, what am I going to do with the prayer style of my inculturation, sit down and be quiet? I say this, I say this to my sisters: "I pray with you in your way for 363 days of the year, but when I ask you that one day to pray my way you look me in the eye and say, 'Well, I'm just really not familiar and this is just not my way. I'm just not comfortable. You know we can't do that.'" Are you with me, Church? We come to your meetings, sometimes. We have been inculturated in a black community that says it is good to have an opinion. It is good to advance that opinion, strenuously, because ideas are clarified in dialogue and the community reaches good decisions when everybody lays the cards on the table and persists in dialogue and planning until we come to satisfying conclusions. What happens in your formation meeting when the black candidate says forcefully and passionately what's on her mind? Sometimes you send her into psychiatric affiliation.

Inculturated in a community in which feelings and passions and emotions are not to be suppressed or repressed or denied, but to be channeled and directed and used to give life to the individual and to the family and to the community and to the church and to the world, the black candidate is expected to sit on his feelings so he won't hurt yours. And my Asian brothers and sisters, trained in respect and control sit there sending out all kinds of non-verbal signals and are criticized for silence, "Well they just won't communicate." If you've heard it, say *Amen*.

I'm talking about sharing life. To what extent are you, to what extent are the members of your congregation really prepared for multicultural living, the give and take of it, thrive and learn of it, the challenge of it? Do we love one another enough as God's children to wait for the miracle of transformation that God's glory may be revealed in us. . . .

To what extent are you ready to eat, to pray, to play, to work with the people of the universe? And if you haven't got time to play with us, to put your feet under the table and rest yourself a while, it is unlikely that you can share faith, life and love with us. Jesus had time to spend at the wedding feast. He and his disciples were there because it was important to be there. And before we leave this feast, let us pray the prayer that Jesus gave. You know the words of this one. (*Our Father—sung*).

We have come together in Jesus' name and we pray Oh Father, give us the spirit of transformation that the water of our lives may become purest wine and that your glory may be revealed to all the brothers and sisters, to the whole cosmos to the limits of the universe. God's glory is revealed because we love one another across the barriers and boundaries of race, culture and class. We love not just in words but in food and in prayer and in song and dance and in learning and working together. *(Music)*

Let the Church say *Amen.*

Notes

Charles de Foucauld

[1] From *Memories of Charles de Foucauld, Explorer and Hermit, Seen in His Letters*, tr. Donald Atwater (London: Burns Oates and Washborn, Ltd., 1938) 37–39, 108–13, 155.

Teilhard de Chardin

[1] Jessica Powers to Margaret Ellen Traxler, Feast of St. Aloysius, 1961. Marquette University Archives.

[2] Pierre Teilhard de Chardin, *Christianity and Evolution*, tr. Rene Hague (New York: Harcourt Brace Jovanovich, Inc., 1969) 91–95.

[3] Pierre Teilhard de Chardin, *The Divine Milieu: An Essay on the Interior Life*, tr. Bernard Wall (New York: Harper & Brothers Publishers, 1960) 17–24.

Giovanni Battista Montini (Pope Paul VI)

[1] Paul VI *Insegnamenti*, 1972, 662 as quoted by Peter Hebblethwaite, *Paul VI: The First Modern Pope* (New York: Paulist Press, 1993) 329.

Dorothy Day

[1] Dorothy Day, *The Long Loneliness* (Garden City, N.Y.: Doubleday Image Books, 1959) 74.

[2] Dorothy Day, *From Union Square to Rome* (Silver Spring, Md.: Preservation of the Faith Press, 1942) 11–13.

[3] Dorothy Day, "More About Holy Poverty, Which is Voluntary Poverty" *The Catholic Worker* (February 1945) 1–2 (http://www.catholicworker.org/dorothyday).

[4] Dorothy Day, "The Scandal of the Works of Mercy" *Commonweal* (4 November 1949) 99–102.

Jessica Powers

[1] Jessica Powers, Letter to Margaret Ellen Traxler, S.S.N.D., Feast of St. Peter Claver, 1961.

162   *Notes*

² Jessica Powers, Letter to Margaret Ellen Traxler, S.S.N.D., February 3, 1963.

³ Jessica Powers, Letter to Margaret Ellen Traxler, S.S.N.D., December 15, 1965. Marquette University Archives.

⁴ Jessica Powers, Letter to Margaret Ellen Traxler, S.S.N.D., July 7, 1965. Marquette University Archives.

Franz Jägerstätter

¹ Coincidentally a year to the day after the death of Edith Stein at Auschwitz.

² From Gordon Zahn, *In Solitary Witness*, rev. ed. (Springfield, Ill.: Templegate Publishers, 1986) 33.

³ Gordon C. Zahn, "In Celebration of Martyrdom" *America* (February 19, 1994) 8–10, 9.

Teresa of Calcutta

¹ Malcolm Muggeridge, *Something Beautiful for God* (New York: Harper & Row, 1971) 18.

² Ibid. 85.

³ Ibid. 91.

⁴ Ibid. 97.

⁵ Ibid. 73–74.

⁶ *In My Own Words*. Compiled by Jose Luis Gonzalez-Balado. (Liguori, Mo.: Liguori Publications, 1996) 40.

⁷ Ibid. 23.

⁸ Ibid. 44.

Thomas Merton

¹ Thomas Merton, *The Seven Storey Mountain* (San Diego and New York: Harcourt Brace Jovanovich, Publishers, 1948, 1976) 3.

² Thomas Merton, *The Seven Storey Mountain* (San Diego and New York: Harcourt Brace Jovanovich, Publishers, 1948, 1976) 410.

³ Monica Furlong, *Merton: A Biography* (San Francisco: Harper & Row, 1985) 314.

⁴ Thomas Merton, *A Vow of Conversation: Journals 1964–1965*, ed. by Naomi Burton Stone (New York: Farrar, Straus, Giroux, 1988) 142.

⁵ Thomas Merton, *The Seven Storey Mountain* (San Diego and New York: Harcourt Brace Jovanovich, Publishers, 1948, 1976) 418–19.

⁶ Thomas Merton, "Contemplation in a World of Action" in *Contemplation in a World of Action* (Garden City, N.Y.: Image Books, 1973) 172–79.

⁷ Thomas Merton, "Integrity" in *Seeds of Contemplation* (New York: New Directions, 1949) 66–67.

[8] Thomas Merton, "We Are One Man" in *New Seeds of Contemplation* (New York: New Directions, 1961) 64–65.

[9] Thomas Merton, "The Annunciation" in *The Collected Poems of Thomas Merton* (New York: New Directions, 1997) 284–85.

Roger of Taizé

[1] Brother Roger as quoted by Kathryn Spink, 28.

[2] As quoted by Kathryn Spink, 35.

[3] Brother Roger as quoted by Kathryn Spink, 43.

[4] Brother Roger of Taizé, *No Greater Love: Sources of Taizé* (Taizé: Ateliers et Presses de Taizé, 1990; Collegeville: The Liturgical Press, 1991) 55.

[5] Brother Roger of Taizé, *No Greater Love*, 20–21

[6] Brother Roger of Taizé, *No Greater Love*, 48.

[7] Brother Roger of Taizé, *No Greater Love*, 48.

Oscar Romero

[1] James R. Brockman, *The Word Remains: A Life of Oscar Romero* (Maryknoll, N.Y.: Orbis Books, 1982) 29.

[2] *The Violence of Love: The Pastoral Wisdom of Archbishop Oscar Romero*, tr. James R. Brockman (San Francisco: Harper & Row, 1982) December 5, 1977, 18.

[3] From *The Violence of Love: The Pastoral Wisdom of Archbishop Oscar Romero*, compiled and trans. by James R. Brockman (San Francisco: Harper & Row Publishers, 1988) 11.

[4] Oscar Romero, *Voice of the Voiceless: The Four Pastoral Letters and Other Statements*, Michael J. Walsh, trans. (Maryknoll, N.Y.: Orbis Books, 1985) 97–99, 115.

[5] From *Orientacion, April 13, 1980,* as quoted by James R. Brockman in *Romero: A Life* (Maryknoll, N.Y.: Orbis Books, 1989) 248 (rev. ed. of *The Word Remains: A Life of Oscar Romero* [Maryknoll, N.Y.: Orbis Books, 1982]).

[6] Document #142. Oscar Romero, "The Poverties of the Beatitudes," Ita Ford, trans., December 1, 1980. Maryknoll Mission Archives.

Jean Vanier

[1] Jean Vanier, *Our Journey Home* (Maryknoll, N.Y.: Orbis Books, 1997) vii.

[2] Jean Vanier, *Our Journey Home*, x.

[3] Jean Vanier, *Our Journey Home,* x.

[4] Charter of the Communities of L'Arche, May, 1993. http://www.larchecanada.org.

[5] Canadian Broadcasting Corporation Interview, July 7, 1997.

[6] Jean Vanier, *Our Journey Home*, xvi.

⁷ Jean Vanier, *Followers of Jesus* (New York: Paulist Press, 1976) 31–32.

⁸ Jean Vanier, *Community and Growth: Our Pilgrimage Together* (New York: Paulist Press, 1979) 1–19.

⁹ Jean Vanier, *From Brokenness to Community* (Mahwah, N.J.: Paulist Press, 1992) 18–19.

Thea Bowman

¹ Thea Bowman, "No Neutral Ground" *Proceedings 1987 Religious Formation Conference National Congress*, 1–12, 3.

Bibliography

Thea Bowman

Almost Home: Living with Suffering and Dying. Ligouri Publishing Co., 1989. Audiocassette.

Families: Black and Catholic, Catholic and Black. Ed. Thea Bowman. Washington, D.C.: U.S. Catholic Conference, 1985.

Sister Thea: Her Own Story. Belleville, Ill.: Oblate Media and Communications. 1991. Videocassette.

Sister Thea: Round the Glory Manger. Boston: Krystal Records, 1989.

Sister Thea: Songs of My People. Boston: Krystal Records, 1988.

Shooting Star: Selected Writings and Speeches. Ed. Celestine Cepress. Winona, Minnesota, 1993.

Old-Time Religion. Loveland, Ohio: Treehaus Communications, 1988. Four Videocassettes.

Dorothy Day

Dorothy Day and the Catholic Worker: A Bibliography and Index. Anne Klejment, Alice Klejment. New York: Garland Press, 1986.

Dorothy Day: Selections from Her Writings. Ed. Michael Garvey. Springfield, Ill.: Templegate Publishers, 1996.

By Little and By Little: The Selected Writings of Dorothy Day. Ed. Robert Ellsberg. New York: Knopf, 1983. Reprinted as *Dorothy Day: Selected Writings.* Maryknoll, N.Y.: Orbis Books, 1992.

From Union Square to Rome. Silver Spring, Md.: Preservation of the Faith Press, 1938, 1940; New York: Arno Press, 1978.

House of Hospitality. New York: Sheed & Ward, 1939.

Loaves and Fishes. New York: Curtis Books, 1963, 1972; San Francisco: Harper & Row, 1983; Maryknoll, N.Y.: Orbis Books, 1997.

The Long Loneliness: The Autobiography of Dorothy Day. New York: Harper, 1952; Garden City, N.Y.: Image Books, 1959; New York: Curtis Books, 1972; San Francisco: Harper & Row, 1983.

Meditations. Selected and arranged by Stanley Vishnewski. New York: Paulist Press, 1970.

On Pilgrimage: The Sixties. New York: Curtis Books, 1972.

Therese. Springfield, Ill.: Templegate, 1979.

Charles de Foucauld

La Bonté de Dieu: Méditations sur les Saints Évangiles. Paris: Nouvelle Cité, 1996.

Cahiers Charles de Foucauld, Grenoble: Arthaud, 1946.

Carnet de Beni Abbes. Paris: Nouvelle Cite, 1993.

Cette Chère Derniere Place: Lettres a Mes Frères de la Trappe. Paris: Cerf, 1991.

Come, Let Us Sing a Song Unknown: Prayers of Charles de Foucauld. First American Edition. Denville, N.J.: Dimension Books, 1900, 1978.

Dictionnaire Touareg-Français: Dialecte de l'Ahaggar. Paris: Imprimerie Nationale de France, 1951.

Écrits Spirituels de Charles de Foucauld: Ermite au Sahara, Apôtre des Touaregs, Quatorzième ed. Paris: J. De Digord, 1964.

Hope in the Gospels. (En Vue De Dieu Seul.) Tr. Nelly Marans. New York: New City Press, 1990.

Inner Search. (Lettres a Mes Frères de La Trappe. Paris: Cerf, 1970.) Tr. Barbara Lucas. Maryknoll, N.Y.: Orbis Books, 1977, 1979.

L'Évangile Presente au Pauvres du Sahara: Petite Introduction au Catechisme. Rabat: Imprimerie Foch, 1938.

L'évangile Présente aux Pauvres Nègres du Sahara. Grenoble: B. Arthaud, 1947.

Lettres à Henry de Castries. Paris: Grasset, 1952.

Lettres à Mme de Bondy, de la Trappe a Tamanrasset. 2nd ed. Paris: Desclee, De Brower, 1967.

Memories of Charles de Foucauld, Explorer and Hermit, Seen in His Letters. George Gorree. Tr. Donald Attwater. Great Britain: Burns Oates & Washbourne, Ltd., 1938.

Meditations of a Hermit. (Trans. from Écrits Spiritueles) Tr. Charlotte Balfour. N.Y.: Orbis Books, 1981.

Œvres Spirituelles. Paris: Nouvelle Cite, 1973.

Poesies Touaregues: Dialecte de L'Ahaggar. Paris: Libraires E. Leroux, 1930.

Reconnaisance au Maroc, 1883–1884. Paris: Socete d'Ed. geographiques, maritimes et coloniales, 1888.

Reconnaissance au Maroc, 1883–1884. Plan-de-la-tour: Ed. d'Aujourd'hui, 1985.

XXV Lettres Inédites du Père de Foucauld. Paris: Bonne Presse, 1946.

Spiritual Autobiography of Charles de Foucauld. Ed. Jean-Francois Six. Tr. J. Holland Smith. New York: P.J. Kenedy, 1964.

Franz Jägerstätter

Gefangnisbriefe und Aufzeichungen: Franz Jägerstätter verweigert 1943 den Wehrdienst. Linz: Veritas, 1987.

Er folgte seinem Gewissen: das einsame Zeugnis des Franz Jägerstätter. Graz: Styria, 1988.

Benesch, Kurt. *Die Suche nach Jägerstätter.* Graz: Styria, 1993.

Kent, Bruce. *Franz Jägerstätter.* London: Catholic Truth Society, 1976.

Putz, Erna. *Franz Jägerstätter.* Linz: Veritas-Verlag, 1985.

Zahn, Gordon. *In Solitary Witness: The Life and Death of Franz Jägerstätter.* Springfield, Ill.: Templegate Publishers, 1964, 1986. (Includes writings of Franz Jägerstätter.)

Thomas Merton

The Ascent to Truth. New York: Harcourt, Brace, Jovanovich, 1951, 1979, 1981.

The Asian Journal of Thomas Merton. Ed. N. Burton, P. Hart, J. Laughlin. New York: New Directions Pub. Corp., 1973.

At Home in the World: The Letters of Thomas Merton & Rosemary Radford Reuther. Ed. Mary Tardiff. Maryknoll, N.Y.: Orbis Books, 1995.

A Catch of Anti-Letters: Thomas Merton, Robert Lax. Mission, Ks.: Sheed, Andrews, McNeel, 1978.

Bread in the Wilderness. Collegeville: The Liturgical Press; Philadelphia: Fortress Press, 1953, 1986.

The Collected Poems of Thomas Merton. New York: New Directions, 1977.

Conjectures of a Guilty Bystander. Garden City, N.Y.: Doubleday, 1966.

Contemplation in a World of Action. Garden City, N.Y.: Doubleday, 1971.

Contemplative Prayer. New York: Herder and Herder, 1969; New York: Image Books, 1992.

The Courage for Truth: Letters to Writers. Ed. Christine M. Bochen. New York: Farrar, Strauss & Giroux, 1993.

Dancing in the Water of Life: Seeking Peace in the Hermitage. (Journals, v. 5) Ed. Robert E. Daggy. San Francisco: Harper, 1997.

Day of a Stranger. Salt Lake City: Gibbs M. Smith, 1981.

Disputed Questions. San Diego: Harcourt, Brace, Jovanovich, 1960, 1985.

Entering the Silence: Becoming a Monk and Writer. (Journals, V. 2) Ed. Jonathan Montaldo. San Francisco: Harper, 1996.

Faith and Violence; Christian Teaching and Christian Practice. Notre Dame, Ind.: University of Notre Dame Press, 1968.

Figures for an Apocalypse. (Poems) Norfolk, Ct.: New Directions, 1947, 1948.

Geography of Holiness: the Photography of Thomas Merton. Ed. D. P. Patnaik. New York: Pilgrim Press, 1980.

The Geography of Lograire. (Poems) New York: New Directions Pub. Corp., 1969.

The Hidden Ground of Love: the Letters of Thomas Merton on Religious Experience and Social Concerns. Ed. William M. Shannon. San Diego: Harcourt, Brace, Jovanovich, 1993.

Honorable Reader: Reflections on My Work. Ed. Robert E. Daggy. New York: Crossroad, 1989. (Revised and expanded ed. of Introductions East & West. Greensboro, N.C.: Unicorn Press, 1981).

The Last of the Fathers: Saint Bernard of Clairvaux and the Encyclical Letter, Doctor Mellifluous. New York: Harcourt Brace Jovanovich, 1954, 1981; Westport, Ct.: Greenwood Press, 1970

Learning to Love: Exploring Solitude and Freedom. Ed. Christine M. Bochen. (Journals, v. 6) San Francisco: Harper, 1997.

Life and Holiness. New York: Herder and Herder, 1963; New York: Doubleday, 1990.

The Literary Essays of Thomas Merton. Ed. Patrick Hart. New York: New Directions, 1981.

The Living Bread. New York: Farrar, Strauss and Giroux, 1956, 1980.

A Man in the Divided Sea. (Poems) Norfolk, Ct.: New Directions, 1946.

The Monastic Journey. Ed. Patrick Hart. Mission, Kansas: Sheed, Andrews, and McNeel, 1977.

Monks Pond: Thomas Merton's Little Magazine. Ed. Robert E. Daggy. Lexington, Ky.: University Press of Kentucky, 1989.

My Argument with the Gestapo; A Macaronic Journal. Garden City, N.Y.: Doubleday, 1969.

Mystics and Zen Masters. New York, Farrar, Strauss and Giroux, 1967.

New Seeds of Contemplation. Norfolk, Ct.: New Directions, 1961, 1962.

No Man is an Island. New York: Harcourt Brace, 1955; New York: Octagon Books, 1983.

The Nonviolent Alternative. Ed. Gordon Zahn. New York: Farrar, Strauss & Giroux, 1971, 1980.

Opening the Bible. Collegeville, Minn.: The Liturgical Press; Philadelphia, Pa.: Fortress Press, 1986.

Original Child Bomb: Points for Meditation to be Scratched on the Walls of a Cave. New York: New Directions, 1962.

The Road to Joy: The Letters of Thomas Merton to New and Old Friends. San Diego: Harcourt Brace Jovanovich, 1993.

Run to the Mountain: The Story of a Vocation. (Journals, v. 1) Ed. Patrick Hart. San Francisco: Harper, 1995.

The School of Charity: the Letters of Thomas Merton on Religious Renewal and Spiritual Direction. Ed. Patrick Hart. New York: Farrar, Straus, Giroux, 1990.

A Search for Solitude: Pursuing the Monk's True Life. (Journals, v. 3) Ed. Lawrence S. Cunningham. San Francisco: Harper, 1996.

Seasons of Celebration. New York: Farrar, Straus and Giroux, 1965.

The Secular Journal of Thomas Merton. London: Sheldon Press, 1959, 1977.

Seeds of Contemplation. Westport, Ct.: Greenwood Press, 1949, 1979.

Seeds of Destruction. New York: Farrar, Strauss and Giroux, 1964, 1965.

Selected Poems. Eleventh ed. New York: New Directions Pub. Corp., 1967.

The Seven Storey Mountain. San Diego: Harcourt Brace Jovanovich, 1948, 1990; New York: Octagon Books, 1976, 1978.

The Sign of Jonas. New York: Harcourt Brace, 1953; Garden City, N.Y.: Image Books, 1956; New York: Octagon Books, 1983.

The Silent Life. New York: Farrar, Straus and Giroux, 1957, 1981.

The Strange Islands (Poems). New York: New Directions, 1957.

Thomas Merton and James Laughlin: Selected Letters. Ed. D. D. Cooper. New York: W. W. Norton, 1997.

Thomas Merton: Early Poems/1940–42. Lexington, Ky.: Anvil Press, 1971.

Thomas Merton on St. Bernard. Kalamazoo, Mi.: Cistercian Publications, 1980.

Thomas Merton in Alaska: prelude to the Asian journal: the Alaskan conferences, journals, and letters. New York: New Directions Pub. Corp., 1989.

Thomas Merton: a preview of the Asian journey. New York: Crossroad, 1989.

Turning Toward the World: The Pivotal Years. (Journals, v. 4) Ed. Victor A. Kramer. San Francisco: Harper, 1996.

A Vow of Conversation: Journals, 1964–1965. New York: Farrar, Strauss, Giroux, 1988.

The Waters of Siloe. New York: Harcourt Brace, 1949, 1979; Garden City, N.Y.: Garden City Books, 1951.

What is Contemplation? Springfield, Ill.: Templegate Publishers, 1981.

The Wisdom of the Desert: Sayings from the Desert Fathers of the Fourth Century. Trans. by Thomas Merton. London: Hollis & Carter, 1961; New Directions, 1970.

Zen and the Birds of Appetite. New York: New Directions, 1968; Boston: Shambhala, 1993.

Giovanni Battista Montini (Paul VI)

The Christian in the Modern World. Tr. Michael M. McManus. London: Burns & Oates, 1963.

The Church. Tr. Alfred Di Lascia. Baltimore: Helicon, 1964.

Dialogues: Reflections on God and Man. Tr. John G. Clancy. New York: Trident Press, 1964, 1965.

Discorsi e scritti sul Concilio (1959–1963), Istituto Paulo VI, Brescia, with Studium, Rome, Quaderni dell'Istituto, 3, 1983. Some of this material is in The Church, Palm Publishers, Montreal, 1964.

Giovanni Battista Montini Arcivescovo de Milano e il Concilio ecumenico Vaticano II, *Preparazione e Primo periodo,* Brescia, 1985.

Lettere a un giovane amico. Ed Cesare Trebeschi. Brescia: Queriniana, 1978.

La preghiera dell'anima, le idee di S. Paolo, Colloqui Religiose, Istituto Paolo VI, Brescia, Quaderni dell'Istituto 1, 1981. Originally published in *Studium,* 1931.

The Mind of Paul VI on the Church and the World. Ed. James Walsh. Tr. Archibald Colquhoun. Milwaukee: Bruce, 1964.

Pope Paul and Christian Unity. Ed. Titus Cranny. Garrison, N.Y.: Chair of Unity Apostolate, 1964–1966.

Populorum Progresso. Boston: Daughters of St. Paul, 1967.

Scritti giovanili. Brescia: Queriana, 1979.

Sulla Madonna, discoursi e scritti 1955–1963. Ed. Rene Laurentin, Studium, Rome and Istituto Paolo VI, Brescia, 1988.

Jessica Powers

The House at Rest. Pewaukee, Wis.: Carmelite Monastery, 1984.

Journey to Bethlehem. Pewaukee, Wis.: Carmelite Monastery, 1972.

The Lantern Burns. New York: Monastire Press, 1939.

The Little Alphabet. Milwaukee: Carmelite Monastery, 1955.

Mountain Sparrow. Reno: Carmelite Monastery, 1972.

The Place of Splendor. New York: Cosmopolitan Science & Art Source Co., 1946.

Selected Poetry of Jessica Powers. Ed. Regina Siegfried and Robert F. Morneau. Kansas City: Sheed & Ward, 1989.

Oscar Romero

A Martyr's Message of Hope: Six Homilies. Kansas City, Mo.: 1981.

Voice of the Voiceless: The Four Pastoral Letters and Other Statements. Tr. Michael J. Walsh. Maryknoll, N.Y.: Orbis Books, 1985.

The Violence of Love: The Pastoral Wisdom of Archbishop Oscar Romero. Tr. James R. Brockman. San Francisco: Harper & Row, 1988.

Romero, Martyr for Liberation: The Last Two Homilies of Archbishop Romero of San Salvador, London: Catholic Institute for International Relations, 1982.

Teilhard de Chardin

Accomplir l'homme. Paris: B. Grasset, 1968.

Activation of Energy. (*Activation de l'énergie.*) Tr. Rene Hague. New York: Harcourt Brace Jovanovich, 1970, 1971.

The Appearance of Man. (*L'apparition de l'homme.* Paris: Éditions du Seuil, 1956.) Tr. J. M. Cohen. New York: Harper & Row, 1965.

Building the Earth. (*Construire la terre.* Paris: Éditions du Seuil, 1958.) Tr. Noel Lindsay. Wilkes-Barre, Pa.: Dimension Books, 1965.

Christianity and Evolution. (*Comment je crois.* Paris: Éditions du Seuil, 1969.) Tr. Rene Hague. London: Collins, 1969. (Also published as *How I Believe.* San Francisco: Harper & Row, 1969); New York: Harcourt Brace Jovanovich, 1971, 1974.

The Divine Milieu: An Essay on the Interior Life. (*Le Milieu divin: essai de vie intérieure.* Paris: Editions du Seuil, 1957.) New York: Harper, 1960.

Early Man in China. New York: AMS Press, 1980.

Être plus. Paris: Editions du Seuil, 1968.

The Future of Man. (*L'avenir de l'homme.* Paris: Éditions du Seuil, 1959.) Tr. Norman Denny. New York: Harper & Row, 1964.

Génése d'une pensée. Paris: B. Grasset, 1961.

The Heart of the Matter. (*Le Cœur de la matière.* Paris: Éditions du Seuil, 1976) Tr. Rene Hague. New York: Harcourt Brace Jovanovich, 1978, 1979, 1980.

Human Energy. (*L'énergie humaine.* Paris: Éditions du Seuil, 1962.) Tr. J. M. Cohen. London: Collins, 1969; New York: Harcourt Brace Jovanovich, 1971.

Hymn of the Universe. (*Hymne de l'univers.* Paris: Éditions de Seuil, 1967.) Tr. Simon Bartholomew. New York: Harper & Row, 1965, 1969.

Je m'explique. Paris: Editions du Seuil, 1966.

La messe sûr le monde. Paris: Editions du Seuil, 1965.

La prêtre. Paris: Editions du Seuil, 1968.

Les cahiers. Paris: Seuil, 1958.

Letters from a Traveler. (*Lettres de voyage, 1923–1939* and *Nouvelles letters de voyage, 1939–1955.* Paris: F. Maspero, 1982) London: Collins, 1962; San Francisco: Harper & Row, 1962.

Letters from Hastings, 1908–1912. (*Lettres d'Hastings et de Paris, 1908–1914.*) New York: Herder & Herder, 1968.

Letters from My Friend, Teilhard de Chardin, 1948–1955. (*Lettres familieres de Pierre Teilhard de Chardin, Mon Ami: Les Dernieres Années, 1948–*

1955. Paris: Centurion, 1976.) Collected by Pierre Leroy. Tr. Mary Lukas. New York: Paulist Press, 1980.

The Letters of Teilhard de Chardin and Lucile Swan. Ed. Thomas M. King and Mary Wood Gilbert. Washington, D.C.: Georgetown University Press, 1993.

Letters to Two Friends, 1926–1952. New York: New American Library, 1968.

Letters to Leontine Zanta. Tr. Bernard Wall. London: Collins, 1969; New York: Harper & Row, 1969.

Lettres à Jeanne Mortier. Paris: Seuil, 1984.

Lettres à l'abbé Gaudefroy et à l'abbé Breuil. Monaco: Éditions du Rocher, 1988.

Letters from Egypt, 1905–1908. (*Lettres d'Egypte, 1905–1908*. Paris: Aubier, 1963.) New York: Herder & Herder, 1965.

The Making of a Mind: Letters form a Soldier-Priest, 1914–1919. New York: Harper & Row, 1965.

Man's Place in Nature: The Human Zoological Group. (*La Place de L'homme dans la Nature: Groupe Zoologique Humain*.) Tr. Rene Hague. New York: Harper & Row, 1966.

Mon univers. Paris: Éditions du Seuil, 1965.

On Happiness. (*Sur le bonheur*. Paris: Éditions du Seuil, 1966.) London: Collins, 1973.

On Love. (*Sur l'amour*. Paris: Éditions du Seuil, 1967.) London: Collins, 1972; New York: Harper & Row, 1972.

On Love and Happiness. San Francisco: Harper & Row, 1984.

On Suffering. (*Sur la souffrance*.) London: Collins, 1975; New York: Harper & Row, 1974.

Réflexions sur le progrès. Peking, 1941.

Science and Christ. (*Science et Christ*.) Tr. Rene Hague. London: Collins, 1968; San Francisco: Harper & Row, 1968.

The Phenomenon of Man. (*La phénomenon humain*. Paris: Éditions du Seuil, 1970.) Tr. Bernard Wall. San Francisco: Harper & Row, 1959, 1965.

Pierre Teilhard de Chardin et Jean Boussac: Lettres de Guerre Inédites. Pr. Francois Guillaumont. Paris: O.E.I.L., 1986.

Toujours en avant. Paris: Desclée, 1970.

Toward the Future. (*Les Directions de L'Avenir*. Paris: Éditions du Seuil, 1973.) Tr. Rene Hague. New York: Harcourt Brace Jovanovich, 1974, 1975; London: Collins, 1975.

The Vision of the Past. (*La vision du passe.* Paris: Éditions du Seuil, 1957). Tr. J. M. Cohen. London: Collins, 1966.

Writings in Time of War. (*Écrits du temps de la guerre: 1916–1919.* Paris: Éditions du Seuil, 1965, 1976). Tr. Rene Hague. London: Collins, 1968; New York: Harper & Row, 1968.

Teresa of Calcutta

A Life for God. Ann Arbor, Mich.: Servant Publications, 1995.

A Gift for God. London: Collins, 1975; New York: Harper & Row, 1975, 1996.

A Simple Path. Ballantine Books, 1995.

Heart of Joy. Ann Arbor, Mich.: Servant Books, 1987.

In My Own Words. Thorndike, Me.: G.K. Hall, 1996; Ligouri, Mo.: Ligouri Publications, 1996.

In the Heart of the World. Novato, Calif.: New World Library, 1997.

In the Silence of the Heart. London: SPCK, 1983.

Jesus, The Word to Be Spoken. New York: Phoenix Press, 1986, 1987.

Life in the Spirit. San Francisco: Harper & Row, 1983.

Love, A Fruit Always in Season. San Francisco: Ignatius Press, 1987.

Loving Jesus, Ann Arbor, Mich.: Servant Publications, 1991.

Mary, Mother of Reconciliations. New York: Paulist Press, 1989.

Meditations from a Simple Path. New York: Ballantine Books, 1996.

Meditations on the Way of the Cross. (*Kreuzweg.*) With Frere Roger Schutz. New York: Pilgrim Press, 1987.

My Life for the Poor. Ed. Jose Luis Gonzales-Balado and Janet N. Playfoot. San Francisco: Harper & Row, 1985.

No Greater Love. New York: Walker and Co., 1997.

One Heart Full of Love. Ann Arbor, Mich.: Servant Books, 1988.

Seeking the Heart of God. San Francisco: HarperSanFrancisco, 1993.

The Best Gift Is Love. Ann Arbor, Mich.: Servant Publications, 1993.

The Blessings of Love. Ann Arbor, Mich.: Charis, 1996.

The Love of Christ. San Francisco: Harper & Row, 1982.

The Joy in Loving. New Delhi: Viking, 1996.

Total Surrender. New York: Walker and Co., 1993.

Words to Love By. Notre Dame, Ind.: Ave Maria Press, 1983.

Brother Roger of Taizé (Roger Schutz)

Afire With Love: Meditations on Peace and Unity. Tr. Emily Chisholm and the Taize Community. New York: Crossroad, 1981, 1982.

The Power of the Provisional (Dynamique du provisoire.) Philadelphia: Pilgrim Press, 1969.

Meditations on the Way of the Cross. (Kreuzweg.) With Mother Teresa of Calcutta. New York: Pilgrim Press, 1987.

This Day Belongs to God. Tr. J.C. Dickinson. London: Faith Press, Baltimore: Helicon Press, 1961.

Unity: Man's Tomorrow. (L'unite: Espérance de vie) London: Faith Press, 1962.

Jean Vanier

An Ark for the Poor: The Story of L'Arche. (L'histoire de l'Arche.) Ottawa: Novalis, 1995.

A Network of Friends: The Letters of Jean Vanier to the Friends and Communities of L'Arche. Ed. John Sumarah. Hantsport, N.S.: Lancelot Press, 1994.

Be Not Afraid. New York: Paulist Press, 1975.

The Broken Body. Mahwah, N.J.: Paulist Press, 1988.

Community and Growth: Our Pilgrimage Together. (Communauté, lieu du pardon et de la fête). Tr. Ann Shearer. Toronto: Griffin House, 1979; London: Darton, Longman, Todd, 1979; New York: Paulist Press, 1979; Bombay: St. Paul Publications, 1991.

Eruption to Hope. Toronto: Griffin House, 1971.

Followers of Jesus. (Disciples de Jesus. Paris: Fleurus, 1977). Toronto: Griffin House; New York: Paulist Press, 1976.

From Brokenness to Community. Mahwah, N.J.: Paulist Press, 1992.

The Heart of L'Arche: A Spirituality for Everyday. Toronto, Ont.: Novalis; New York: Crossroad, 1995.

In Weakness, Strength: The Spiritual Sources of Georges P. Vanier, 19th Governor-General of Canada. Toronto: Griffin House, 1969.

Jesus, The Gift of Love. New York: Crossroad, 1994.

Man and Woman He Made Them. (Homme et femme Il les fit). Mahwah, N.J.: Paulist Press, 1985.

Our Journey Home; Rediscovering a Common Humanity Beyond Our Differences (Toute personne est une histoire sacreé. Ottawa, Ont.: Novalis;

Paris: Plon, 1994.) Tr. Maggie Parham. Maryknoll, N.Y.: Orbis, 1997.

Ouvre mes bras. Paris: Fleurus, 1973.

Tears of Silence. Toronto: Griffin House, 1970.